Table of Contents

Part One: Motivation, Preparation, Education, Inspiration

Part Two: Perspiration, Innovation, Dedication

I PERSPIRATION

Building Your Inventory

The First Three Keys to Success: Factor in Pricing, Sales Rank, and Availability

Pricing

The Fourth Key to Success: Competitive Pricing

I MOTIVATION

How the Global Marketplace Changed the Face of Small Businesses for Stay-at-Home Moms

If you're reading this guide looking for a low risk way to make a transition from the traditional 9-5 "on the clock" approach to making money, to the flexibility of running your own business, then you've come to the right place. On the other hand, if you're an established bookseller, looking for fresh ideas, feel free to move on to parts one and two while I spend a few minutes raving about the unprecedented opportunities that have come with our ability to connect to a worldwide marketplace from home.

Although my tendency is to think that everyone should quite naturally share in my enthusiasm, I can certainly understand why many stay-at-home moms have abandoned the idea of living a more synthesized life, especially if success has evaded you in the past. In fact, before stumbling upon this opportunity, my ability to bridge the gap between home and work seemed an elusive, unattainable goal. I was stuck between two values--work and family--both good, yet seemingly incompatible. Thus, I had fleeting thoughts of starting my own business. But the idea of start-up-loans, procurement issues, and all the other hassles associated with many small businesses amounted to a superhuman feat of strength--just when I was low on time, energy, and money. Still, I felt a gravitational pull to do something different, vacillating between doubt and hope for a miracle.

Eventually, I gave up on the idea of successfully combining motherhood and work—what I had come to view as a pair of opposites. But I was left with a couple of nagging questions: could the pair ever live in harmony? Was a holistic approach to life remotely possible? One thing was certain. I had to work; yet, I wasn't happy with the job I had or with the idea of starting a full scale business of my own. So I would have to come up with a third alternative.

Ah Ha!

Then it happened. I was at a party, enjoying a lemon drop, when I heard what some assumed was a suburban myth about a stay-at-home mom who had transcended the narrow confines of a work-centered existence by selling used books on Amazon. The way the story went, she made $20,000 the first year, feverishly working at her computer (part-time) in the privacy of her own den.

I couldn't believe it. I wouldn't have to unravel the mysteries of the universe to overcome the conventional constraints imposed upon me by my dependence on a second income. All I needed was a computer, a post office, and a place to find used books. A few organizational skills I'd acquired from watching TV and children at the same time as cooking, talking on the phone, and learning a second language, also came in handy. Of course, it helped that I love books, the thrill of the hunt, a chance bargain, digging for gold, and telling everyone who thought it was just a myth, "I told you so." Which is the first thing I did when I not only made $20,000 my first year selling used books on Amazon, I surpassed it.

What Makes Selling Books on Amazon Such a Low-Risk High-Profit Opportunity?

If you've never heard of the 4 P's of marketing, I'm about to put them in a nutshell to exemplify what makes selling books on Amazon so attractive. The 4 P's of marketing stand for place, product, promotion, and price. Developing a good marketing mix, based on these factors, can be quite complicated, and the inability to do so effectively has been the demise of many potential businesses. But if you stop to think about it, in the case of selling books on Amazon, most of the work has been done for you--with proven success!

By becoming an Amazon Marketplace seller, you are entering into a partnership (so to speak) with the most successful bookseller in the world. You are going to be selling used books, which have tremendous sales potential: almost everyone reads one genre or another, so it is the perfect product. You'll be selling online, which enables you to reach across the globe, 24 hours a day, 7 days a week (place), working under Amazon's brand name (promotion), and selling at a competitive cost, since the books are used (price).

Furthermore, you not only have a readymade proven marketing mix, developed by the most successful bookseller in the world, you have almost no overhead (I store my books in my garage), and you need very little investment income (I started with about $100). So you don't have to wait long before making a profit (I made a profit the first month). It just doesn't get any better than that!

Clearing Up Your Doubts

If you have toddlers clamoring at your feet; dinner boiling over on the stove; a crying baby in need of attention; or someone waiting for a ride to ballet or soccer practice--but no lingering doubts--feel free to bypass this section completely. It won't bother me a bit.

On the other hand, if you're still skeptical about selling used books online, that's not necessarily a bad thing, especially if you've run the gambit of get-rich-quick scams or pyramid schemes that only work for the person on the top (whose identity is still a mystery to me). But don't let that skepticism blind you to a very real opportunity when it comes along.

In the case of selling books on Amazon, there's a lot to rave about. It requires no formal education, no previous experience, little investment cash, and no overhead. Nor is it a gamble, like the hand-painted t-shirts my friend and I tried to sell in New York on weekends after we'd worked a 40-hour week. You don't even have to climb to the top of a pyramid (after deciding where to donate those beautiful hand-painted t-shirts that are now taking up space in your closet).

Most importantly, there's no need to sell those amazing health products to your friends and relatives. You know the products I'm talking about. The ones that make you look and feel young again for only $199 a month. Unless, of course, you become a distributor so you too can get the products wholesale. No, contrary to what those experiences have taught you, this opportunity really works. So, if you'll pardon the exclamation (how can you motivate and inspire without one?), it works for just about anyone and it will work for you!

The Internet Never Sleeps

To emphasize how one of the essential 4P's (place) is going to be working overtime, unlike the rest of us, the Internet never sleeps. So when you're enjoying some of the freedoms that come from structuring your life as you please, your books are selling online, 24 hours a day, seven days a week, reaching across the globe to draw in customers from every time zone and location that has Internet access.

This is ultimately one of the major advantages available to today's stay-at-home moms (or anyone starting a business, for that matter). It is the be-all-and-end-all secret to maximizing your profits while minimizing your efforts. For example, I love the feeling of having dinner with friends, or going to the gym, only to arrive home, click on the Amazon site and discover that I've sold one of my top-dollar $185 to $399 books. Isn't life grand?

Is This Guide Just for Stay-at-Home Moms?

But the advantages of tapping into a global marketplace aren't just for the few. Alternatively, the information contained in this guide is beneficial for anyone who wants to earn a few hundred extra dollars a week, whether you're retired, looking to supplement your income, or just want to increase the sales volume to start a full-scale business of your own. Indeed, one option is to blow up the model provided, earning $6,000 to $10,000 a month (or more), as some super-aggressive booksellers have done. What's the blown up version? Time equals money (assuming you're spending that time wisely). So the more time and energy you put into your business--building a solid inventory of books--the more money you'll make.

Yes, I've taken steps along the way to consider specific concerns of stay-at-home moms, since they must adapt things in creative ways in search of a peaceful coexistence between home, work, and play. But the same information that will be provided to stay-at-home moms will supply anyone interested in starting an online book business with the skill set needed for success. Then it's up to the individual to set the bar as high or low as he or she chooses.

I've also taken steps to make this guide as easy to read as possible, without compromising its efficacy. I probably shouldn't admit this, but I hate reading instructional guides of any kind. Thus, as your consultant, I've presented major strategies, principles, and techniques, embedded in stories, real life examples, graphs, and illustrations, whenever possible. I suspect this will reduce the monotony of processing some of the more tedious information required. For example, here's an illustration depicting the advantages of setting your own hours. For those of you who've longed for teachers' hours--set them for yourself. Take weekends and summers off.

II PREPARATION

Setting Realistic Goals

I hope you're beginning to understand why the opportunities for online booksellers are so attractive. But in contrast to concepts you may have read about in get-rich-quick schemes, this option is not a shortcut to success—it's a path. Naturally, a successful business doesn't burst forth fully developed. On the contrary, making a gradual transition has its advantages, especially if you're nervous about jumping in head first. So the teaching method I've employed takes you on a step-by-step hierarchical journey to success. If you want to accelerate the pace, you can put in the extra effort required. Otherwise, I have taken into account the time constraints placed on many stay-at-home moms and anticipate that you can make roughly $200 to $250 in profit per week (fairly early on in your business), working about 10-15 hours a week.

Step by Step/Hierarchical Method

Keep in mind, the figures I quoted on early earning potential are rough estimates. However, I used my experience to guide me, so those

> **Stay-at-Home Mom Tip #1:** You can make more money selling on multiple Internet sites, as some of the profiles I've included will exemplify. But as a stay at-home mom, I bet you have enough balls in the air already. And selling on multiple sites takes more organization. Thus, I recommend selling on one site (at least for now), and the most profitable I've found is Amazon.

numbers-$200 to $250 a week--reflect my early earnings, starting out small--$100 investment cash--and working and storing books in my den--no overhead costs.

On the other hand, as I began to understand the relationship between the size of my inventory and my profits, I began working longer hours to build my inventory as quickly as possible, making $20,000+ my first year. Once I had too many books to fit in the den, my husband built shelves in the garage (still no overhead costs).

I now have anywhere from 1,000 to 1,200 books in my inventory at any given time. An inventory of this size is not substantial by most standards. In fact, I had accumulated just as many books by the end of my first year selling books on Amazon. But before writing this guide, I decided to purge my inventory of early mistakes and make a fresh start. Rebuilding my inventory, with the advantage of experience, gave me the opportunity to stock it more efficiently. It also helped me to write this guide in a step-by-step fashion. One door closes and another opens!

If you're starting to wonder about the profit potential of an inventory this size, I don't mind revealing a few facts about my own business. My average monthly income has grown to $2,700. I spend about $300 a month on books (working to build my inventory); $70 on service charges for my Sidekick (a mobile lookup tool used to gather information before buying books); $30 on an online postage service; $50 on packing supplies and cappuccino; and $150 on postage. So if you do the math, $2,700-$600 leaves me with $2,100 a month profit (but I'm still growing!). I warned you--it's not a get-rich-quick scheme. But it's a safe, reliable, fun way to harmonize home and work. Thus, the nature and magnitude of change that comes from this synergy is impossible to measure in dollars and cents.

Furthermore, if the income potential cited isn't enough to allow you to leave your 9-5 job, but you're getting excited about the possibility, there's no need to worry since time equals money. I can attest to this based on the results I've had when I increased my hours, since the adage held up. I've made over $4,200 in a month (~$3,300+ in profit) even though I only had between 1,000-1,200 books in my inventory at the time. More impressive are those who make $6,000 to $10,000 a month, working full time and maintaining a substantial inventory.

What kind of inventory brings in profits such as these? Based on my experience, an inventory of about 1,000 to 1,200 books can bring in between $2,000 to $3,000 in monthly profits (as mine has). Thus, an inventory three times that size has the capacity to bring in profits ranging from $6,000 to $9,000 a month, depending on the seller's ability to stock it efficiency and the hours spent in building and maintenance.

I stress efficiency because many booksellers have been impressed by my ability to generate monthly profits of $2,000 to $3,000 with so few books in my inventory. That they are surprised calls for a cautionary word about expecting the same results. Remember, I purged my inventory of early purchase errors and rebuilt it with knowledge and experience. I had also accumulated many top-dollar books, which were starting to sell on a consistent basis (much more about this strategy to come).

I also mention maintenance because you must be out hunting for new books in order to replenish your inventory as you're selling off existing books. Indeed, another factor in my ability to make decent profits with so few books is through a steady flow of sales. During peak profit months, I've found it difficult to keep up, let alone build, a larger inventory.

But by no means is the emphasis on hard work and costly mistakes meant as a discouragement (especially since you're not going to make the same mistakes I made). On the contrary, whether your goal is to make the midrange profits my business generates or to realize the larger profits associated with super-aggressive full time booksellers--it's attainable--others have done it and so can you!

However, it takes a step-by-step approach to reach most goals. And those steps can be riddled with detours and pitfalls. That's why it's important to understand the ground rules and start your business with a plan. Unfortunately, I failed to start with knowledge and direction. Instead, I merely went to garage sales, taking educated guesses as to the resale value of books. But, all that began to change with the weather.

From Garage Sales to Indoor Venues & Search Engines

By the time fall arrived, I had to move indoors. So I visited www.booksalefinder.com to find places in my area that sell used books. Through this resource, I found many ongoing sales sponsored by Friends of the Library. These nonprofit stores, designed to support local libraries, are generally inexpensive, charging an average of fifty-cents to a couple of dollars per book. This is a great way to find a wide variety of books that originate from donations and library discards. By going to the Book Sale Finder site, clicking on your state, then refining your search to nearby locations, you can also find local libraries that have sale shelves set up within the libraries themselves, as part of an ongoing fundraising effort.

Along with ongoing sales, Book Sale Finder lists many large special-occasion book sale events (often sponsored by universities or community organizations). I must admit, I bypass these special-occasion book sales because I prefer to peruse, rather than compete. But don't let that stop you; many scouts make lots of money this way. In fact, I have friends who stock much of their inventory through this venue alone.

However, before competing for books at a large book sale event you, should spend a few months hunting for books at low key venues. The fast-paced environment at big book sales is not for newcomers. You will be up against experienced book scouts who will snatch the best books right out from under you. So wait until you have some experience; then be first in line!

While others are competing for the best buys at large book sale events, I am out purchasing about 40% of my books from several Friends of the Library stores in my area. I buy another 40% in combined purchases from a local Goodwill and my favorite neighborhood thrift store.

Goodwill stores in my area charge an average of $1.99 to $3.99 per book, but in some states Goodwill has a flat rate of one dollar per hardback and fifty cents per paperback. The other 20% of my inventory comes from items purchased at a variety of locations including garage sales, estate sales, local library fundraising shelves, and anywhere else I happen to find them. You will find a complete list in the appendix.

Eventually the cost of buying books begins to add up, even at the cheapest of venues. I have also noticed that some proprietors are increasing the prices of their used books, possibly motivated by book scouts whose buying habits have made them think twice about the resale value of the printed word. So once the weather drove me indoors, beyond the confines of garage sale discounts, I quickly realized that I would have to find a way to determine the resale value of books before making buying decisions. No more buying blind!

Fortunately, you can find all the information needed to make informed buying decisions by going to www.Amazon.com and utilizing Amazon's database to look up books by their ISBN number, title, or author. So that's what I did.

My first method of accessing this information, although not ideal, will work for anyone who doesn't want to invest money before testing the waters. So for those of you who aren't planning on diving in head first, an outline of my earliest technique is as follows: I would go out book scouting, write down the ISBN numbers of promising books, run back home and look them up on my computer. If I found books worth buying, I would rush back to the store in hopes that they would still be sitting on the shelves where I left them.

But my preferred method was to have someone waiting by the phone to look up information for me. This is exactly what I did when my husband was available. He would then tell me the resale value of a book, along with other relevant details (which you'll learn about later), so I could make the best buying decisions. Then I took my business to the next level—I bought a Sidekick.

Note: www.fetchbook.info and www.bookfinder.com are other resources for looking up books. I use Amazon's database, since that's where I sell my books, but I go to bookfinder.com for comparison shopping if I suspect an Amazon price is inflated.

If I Could Do Things Differently

I didn't realize it at the time, but I was about to discover some of the things I could have done differently, which would have saved me lots of time and/or money. One of those things would have been to purchase a mobile lookup device earlier on in my business. For those of you who are unfamiliar with this technology, it is a handheld phone, Sidekick, Blackberry, or scanner with Internet access. These "lookup tools" have web access, allowing you to do some research from remote locations, so you can make the best buying decisions on the spot.

Although I was hyper-cautious about investing money, I have since come to appreciate the interrelationship between my Sidekick and my profit potential. In fact, if I were to wager a guess, I'd bet my Sidekick pays for itself in just one hour of book scouting alone (I go out book-hunting 3-4 days a week for 3-4 hours a day).

Another thing I'd do differently is to utilize the information found, by searching Amazon's database with my mobile lookup device, to stock my inventory with high-dollar books, which can be worth as much as 10-300 times what you pay for them and more. But here's the caveat: these high-dollar books often come with a high sales rank, meaning they are slow sellers, sometimes taking as many as 6 months to a year or more to sell (more about sales ranks later).

So what makes high-dollar/slow-selling books so attractive that they're worth mentioning this early on? I stress buying this particular category of books because they are a great early business strategy based on the profits they will eventually bring your way. It took me far too long to discover this, but once you have enough of these top-dollar books in your inventory you will start selling a few every week, giving your monthly sales a huge jolt. In fact, I like to think of these books like stocks. Since I would pay $2 for a stock, in order to realize a $65 return on my investment within a year or so, I'm also willing to pay $2 for a book that has a good chance of yielding the same return. If I can find 200 books for $3 each (a $600 investment), with a good possibility of yielding anywhere from $8,000 to $15,000 or more in a year's time--all the better. So that's what I did. Then I waited it out until things got started and the momentum began to build.

But before you begin to buy books in this category, you'll need to read some guidelines on how to choose slow-selling books that won't become outdated on your shelves. Just as you wouldn't buy a stock without doing a little research before investing your money, you will also need to learn how to analyze the risks and benefits of this investment. So you'll learn some guidelines in the sections of this guide devoted to finding, recognizing, and selecting books of value.

Another advantage of high-dollar/slow-selling books is that many book scouts pass these books by (as I once did), not realizing the long-term benefits, or simply because they have a different business model. Whatever the reason, they leave top-dollar books sitting on the shelves for the rest of us. But I lacked information when I started my business, which is probably my biggest regret. One of the most significant drawbacks of starting unprepared is that I didn't have enough information to factor in all the variables associated with making good book buying decisions. As you'll soon discover, a book's listing price is a starting point in determining its *real* value, but to make comprehensive buying decisions you will need to learn a lot more.

I would specifically urge you to pay close attention to the sales rank section. As I mentioned, the sales rank, which is calculated by Amazon, tells you how fast a book is likely to sell, partially based on its sales history. Without this information, you have no reference point to help you determine whether or not a book will sell before the supply outweighs the demand, or if the return you will realize on your investment is worth the wait.

Despite its importance, I can't tell you how many times I've talked to new booksellers, often many months into the business, who have no idea what a sales rank is or how to use it when making buying decisions. I think partial responsibility lies in the lack of emphasis placed on this aspect of the business in many earlier books written for used booksellers. Yet lack of knowledge about the role of the sales rank is the main reason I had to purge my inventory of mistakes, sending boxes of books back from whence they came.

Learning from My Mistakes

Obviously, there's no use lamenting about past mistakes. But I mention mine to encourage you not to make the same, including my neglect to start with more information and a basic plan. If you've read any of Stephen Covey's books on the habits of highly successful people, you will find that one of the guiding principles stressed throughout his literature is the need to start with the end in mind.

I understand that many of you are beginning this business uncertain of whether or not you will want to continue long-term. You may doubt its profitability or question if it's right for you. But you will never really know if you can create a successful enterprise unless the steps you take are in the right direction. And the steps you take are directly connected to the extent to which you start with the end in mind.

In the case of selling used books, I am not suggesting the need for a full-scale business plan or big investment. However, I do recommend that you pay close attention to the mistakes I made, especially regarding misunderstandings about how to determine the *true* value of a book, which I could have avoided with a bit more research and preparation.

In the end, if you start your business without some direction, it is like starting a road trip without checking Mapquest to plan the best route. Without a road map it may take you forever to reach your destination--if at all. At a minimum, you will need a compass to guide the way. So do your homework. You'll find the study materials in this guide.

Ideas for Getting Started
If You Can't Afford a Lapse in Your Weekly Income

I hope you're beginning to realize the benefits of a thoughtful approach, so you don't fail by default. I've already mentioned the value of stocking high-dollar/slow-selling books, based on the profits you will realize in the long run--but don't limit yourself. There are many benefits that come from the creation of a diverse buying and selling strategy. This might include stocking some fast-selling/low-profit titles. I don't recommend this category of books as an *overall* strategy for busy stay-at-home moms, since it's so time-consuming to sell low-profit books in the volume needed to make decent profits. But it's a good supplement. It's also a good alternative if you can't afford a lapse in your monthly income when just getting started.

The reason low-profit books are perfect for bringing in early profits is fast turnover and availability. If you divide books into three selling categories: fast, medium, and slow; then also divide them into three profit categories: low, medium, and high, you will begin to understand some of the variables involved in finding used books worth buying and selling. I've already discussed the drawback of many high-dollar books being slow sellers. Now add to this disadvantage the fact that many of the many accessible, fast-selling books have a low profit margin.

However, despite the disadvantages, selling a high-volume of low-profit/fast-selling titles may be a necessary inconvenience when getting started. You may also want to include it as part of a diverse sales model. If possible, it helps to combine this sales strategy with a mobile lookup tool. Having said this, one of the most affordable ways to look up books is with a cell phone that has Internet access and a subscription lookup tool costing about $10 a month. You certainly can't stock a high-volume of fast-selling/low-profit books if you have to run home to look them up on your computer. So, if you can't afford an Internet enabled cell phone, you need someone waiting by the telephone to look up books for you. Or you can buy blind at the lower priced garage sale venue, which is the option of last resort.

Note: Mobile lookup tools will be discussed at length in the section on book-buying tools. Consider the options carefully! A cell phone is the cheapest tool, but it's not the fastest or most efficient. Also, keep in mind, when you see price quotes throughout this book, that they are all time sensitive.

If you're wondering what constitutes a low-profit book, my cutoff for books that will sell within a week is a return of $5 or $6. Also factor in the general rule that you should realize 3 times the return on your investment.

Since it can be easy to forget all the deductions you'll need to consider, I'll give you an example. If you find a book with a listing price of $12, you must deduct $1.80 (Amazon's 15% commission) along with another $1.35 (variable fee), which brings you to $8.85 minus the cost of the book. In this scenario, if the book costs $2, it is within the minimum range of realizing three times your investment. It also hits the minimum $5 or $6 profit mark that I set for my fast-selling books, since the total profit will be $6.85.

Something else to consider is the fact that books fitting into this category may be easy to find because they are on the brink of flooding the market. Good examples would be current self-help and personal growth books; health, fitness, and diet books; and personal finance titles. For example, the book *Rich Dad Poor Dad* was once a quick way to make a small profit, as was *Fit for Life,* and *The Detox Diet.* But these opportunities were short lived.

Thus, time is of the essence when selling books in this category, so you should price them to sell ASAP. This demands that you refresh your inventory on a daily basis, adjusting the prices of your books so that they are listed competitively on an ongoing basis (more about this later). If you don't, the supply may surpass the demand and you may find yourself in a race to the bottom as more and more sellers, also listing these easily accessible copies, undercut your price. You certainly don't want to end up piling books in your closet on top of beautiful hand-painted T-shirts and sample Mary Kay products.

So when your friends, who extolled the virtues of the *Detox Diet* and *Fit for Life* exercise program, start taking strip-aerobics and sipping margaritas on the weekends, it's time to start looking for the next hot topic. After all, everyone knows someone with attention deficit disorder, a hyperactive child, the dream of a weight-loss program that doesn't require cutting back on calories, or the hope of a get-rich-quick plan that really works—or is it just me?

There's More to Buying Books than Knowing the Selling Price

I suspect you're beginning to understand why I said that knowing a book's listing price is just a starting point in determining its *real* value. Indeed, to make comprehensive buying decisions you will need to consider a number of variables. You're now familiar with high-dollar/slow-selling books and low-profit/fast-selling books. Yet there are many possibilities that exist outside these two extremes. And those who employ a diverse buying strategy must have all the information needed to take advantage of the wide variety of books that will cross their paths while out book-hunting.

Connecting all the dots requires the ability to link together important factors about a book's unique characteristics like its price, condition, edition, sales rank, and supply versus demand. But it's going to take awhile to cover each of these variables individually, before bringing them together to make your listing on Amazon as effective as possible in selling your books. Thus, you will have to wait until you finish the section on sales ranks before you can fully appreciate the dynamics of book buying. By then you'll have enough information to fill in the blanks and move forward on your own—equipped to build a profitable inventory of books, once you learn where and how to find them.

Build Your Inventory Before Leaving Your 9-5 Job

Stay-at-Home Mom Tip #3:
If you decide to start making a profit before leaving your 9-5 job, get a babysitter for a few hours on Saturday or Sunday, when people are dropping off their donations and running garage and estate sales.

A good way to learn about the business is to start buying and selling books on the side until you're ready to leave your 9-5 job. This will allow you the ease of building your inventory while bringing in a steady paycheck. In the inspiration section, I profile a man who buys books on his lunch hour, making $9,000 in extra income per year. Working extra hours may be a lot to ask of those who are already exhausted and overextended, but doing so will give you an idea of what to expect. If lunchtime isn't an option, go to Goodwill on Sunday afternoons. This tends to be one of the most profitable days of the week, since so many people drop off their donations on Saturday, and those new books (that haven't been picked over) are often priced and shelved on Sunday and Monday. Just ask the person shelving books how fast new donations hit the sales floor.

This approach will also give you the opportunity to keep track of the hours you spend looking for books to see how much profit you will realize once they sell. Of course, your findings won't be perfect, since you'll be lacking in experience and the flexibility to position yourself in key locations when shelves are being freshly stocked. But if you have clear income objectives, a trial period can be somewhat predictive in helping you determine whether or not you can make enough money to leave your 9-5 job.

Another advantage of this option is that it gives you the opportunity to explore a few different buying and selling strategies and how they best suit your circumstances and the unique opportunities inherent to your geographic location. For example, do you live near a university or industry associated with high quality, valuable, or plentiful reading material? If so, where are the people affiliated with these organizations most likely to donate books? Or, is there a wealthy neighborhood in your area with a nearby Goodwill or thrift store?

This is your opportunity to investigate. Try as many locations as possible within a reasonable distance from your home. Then go to them a few times throughout the day for a couple of weeks. Finding the right buying opportunities will be a key to your success, but it's tricky, since timing is everything. I know book scouts who are convinced that one of my most profitable stores isn't worth the time of day, simply because they dropped in a few times and couldn't find a decent book. So I have it all to myself!

If you decide to test the waters before jumping in, relax and enjoy the benefits. It is a very low-stress/low-risk approach to starting a small business, so you can rest easy. Just be sure to familiarize yourself with important book buying guidelines before you begin and move long-term goals to the forefront as soon as you are confident in your ultimate success.

My Role in the Process

In writing this guide, I took a step-by-step hierarchical approach, perfect for stay-at-home moms but also adaptable to quick starts. I also embedded important information in stories and profiles, with hopes that the whimsical nature of the guide will hold your interest while important information takes root. But I started with motivational/inspirational topics to establish the tremendous possibilities available through this approach. Undoubtedly, each of us writing about the opportunity for online booksellers has a unique point of reference. Thus, we are apt to present particular points or angles in new ways, offering fresh ideas, even handling basic information uniquely.

Further, just as no book scout can cover every nook and cranny of the world--leaving openings for the rest of us--no bookseller knows everything there is to know about every technique, strategy, or genre (with the possible exception of that bookseller in Kabul). Nor can any one writer offer the definitive word on the subject of how to make money by selling books online. That's why continued education is so important. If you don't believe me, take it from Andy McIntyre who said: "If you think that training and education costs too much, try ignorance."

Continuing Education

Because increased knowledge is one of the best predictors of increased earnings, I've read most of the books written for online booksellers. I found it best to buy a variety of books, on the subject of online selling, by a few different authors. This will give you the widest range of viewpoints, tips, techniques and strategies. You must also read the rules set forth by Amazon--don't expect any one book to include all of Amazon's guidelines. Once you have a good foundation in the basics, you might also buy books strictly devoted to areas of special interest. Some topics demand undivided attention. For example, identifying first editions can be trickier than one would expect, since not every publisher uses the same method. But there are a number of books on the subject of first editions, like *The Pocket Guide to the Identification of First Editions* by Bill McBride and Ian Ellis's book entitled, *Book Finds, 3rd Edition: How to Find, Buy, and Sell Used and Rare Books.* You can also buy books on collectibles of almost any genre, from children's books to comics. Just make sure that books focusing on price guidelines are up to date, since the value of collectibles is unstable. In short, educate yourself. It's a business investment.

Etiquette: What I Learned in Kindergarten

Do you remember the book about learning everything you needed to know in kindergarten? The author used the basics of putting things back where you found them, cleaning up your own mess, and playing fair, to make a point about the life-long value of cooperation and respect. These principles also help define the basics of book scout etiquette.

When I first started scouting books, I worked hard to gain the respect of librarians and other proprietors who hadn't warmed up to the idea of anyone perusing their shelves for resale value. More than once, I heard librarians mumbling something under their breath (it is a free market economy, I thought). But I took the time to interact and develop relationships with these critics, treating their efforts with respect by leaving things the way I found them. Eventually they came to understand the value of my high-volume buying. It was a win-win situation, since my high-volume buying boosted their profits as well.

Thus, I have little tolerance for scouts who thwart those efforts by disrupting everything in their path in search of the right book. Or by behaving so badly that some book scouting tools, like scanners, are being banned from many major book sale events (for this reason you should call in advance if you plan on attending one of these events with a scanner). At a recent sale in my area, some book scouts showed up with sheets, using them to cover tables in an attempt to keep books to themselves until they finished looking them up. They also carted books off for private scanning, leaving discarded books scattered about. By the time the next sale came around, scanners were banned and everyone lost. Keep in mind: we should be working to open doors, not close them!

If you were a tourist, preparing to visit a distant land, you might want to have a mental picture of the landscape and its people before hopping on an airplane to make the long flight. In the same vein, specific examples of some of the people working in this field, their backgrounds, business models, and financial returns might help you prepare for the book-hunting journey-- making it easier to judge whether or not the business is right for you. Despite their differences, each of the individuals I've profiled has found a way to build a successful business selling books online. So I offer this visual landscape—drawing on the adage that a picture's worth a thousand words.

Case #1: **Jonathan is a full time computer engineer who supplements his income by buying books at Goodwill on his lunch hour and an occasional weekend.** He then lists books at night, sends them out before work in the morning, and makes about $9,000 a year in extra income. Jonathan specializes in business and computer books, spending 45 minutes of his lunch break looking through the technical section of the Goodwill Store near his work. He uses a cell phone to search Amazon's database for information like pricing, sales rank, and the number of copies available, by plugging in the book's ISBN number (you'll learn how to do this later).

Using an Internet enabled cell phone to look up information and having a specialization is an important part of Jonathan's part-time business model. A cell phone, with Internet access and a subscription "lookup tool," is one of the cheapest ways to access information before buying books. And because his time is limited, having a specialization helps him narrow in on one area, rather than combing through the shelves looking for books of every genre. He also looks at the date on the coded Goodwill price sticker, so he doesn't waste time looking up books that he's already reviewed and rejected.

When I see Jonathan he's always equipped with a Starbucks coffee and an iPod. Although I'm sure he enjoys his music, personally I suspect the iPod is part of an ingenious plot, like carrying a book on a plane, which acts as a buffer to ward off unwanted conversation. If you've never been out book-hunting, you've yet to experience the questions of curious shoppers who want to know all about what you're doing. This is especially inconvenient when you're racing against the clock to find books before other scouts arrive. Furthermore, although it's one thing to give away information in a book that you're sending off to remote locations, it's another thing to reveal your secrets in your own backyard.

However, while I don't object to book props or iPod buffers, if you don't get to know the people working in the stores that you frequent, you're less likely to know important facts, like when the shelves are being stocked. Although it isn't as important for Jonathan to gather information, since he doesn't have the flexibility to adjust his schedule to accommodate the store's routine, other book scouts are well served to make these connections. Furthermore, knowing the staff members who work at the stores on your book-buying route may afford you special considerations. For example, I have been allowed to look through boxes of books before they hit the sales floor. The key is to know how to make the most of your own unique business model.

Case #2: **Pat left a corporate management position to sell books full-time on Amazon and other Internet sites**. If there's one person who could make it to the top of a pyramid scheme, I suspect it would be Pat. Even though he's been selling used books for less than two years, he makes $8,000 to $10,000 a month (66.5% profit and growing), reselling the books he buys at Goodwill, thrift stores, estate sales, garage sales, large book sale events, and anywhere else he happens to find them.

Pat treats his business professionally, charting his growth; looking at sales trends and patterns; and always seeking out new opportunities--like posting on Craigslist and making contacts to preview books before the actual date of an upcoming sale--networking just as he did in the corporate world. He also reads every book on the subject of online selling to keep his competitive edge.

While Pat is the first to queue up at estate sales, his books are first in line at the Amazon Marketplace. Unless you're an established seller, reading this guide for fresh ideas, you haven't yet learned the importance of refreshing your inventory on a daily basis by re-pricing your books to match the competition. In Pat's case, he has the added luxury of a software system that adjusts the prices of his books on an ongoing basis, while he's out hunting down more titles (more about software later).

Pat also works hard to keep his Amazon rating high, which is based on customer feedback. He sends out confirmation emails, works with customers when there's a problem, asks that negative feedback be removed (if he gets any) and offers full and partial returns. He also refuses to sell books if the profit margin is only $5 or $6 because he doesn't like to risk getting a bad review just to make a few bucks. So when buying books his cutoff listing price is a minimum of $17 to $24.

Instead of using a Internet enabled cell phone, Pat uses a scanner which quickly reads the barcodes of books, displaying data that helps him to determine how much a book is worth and how fast it's likely to sell. This method of retrieving information is perfect for Pat's full-scale business model, since it enabled him to build a very large inventory in a very short period of time. His inventory now consists of over 4,000 books. He has also become somewhat of an expert on CD's and makes lots of money buying and selling these as well.

But this no surprise, since he is an overall hardworking, aggressive go-getter with no children, dogs, cats, or plants. Although it is possible to develop a business of this scope by implementing a blown up version of my midrange business model, it's a full time job and a lot of work!

Case #3: **Phillip doesn't sell his books on Amazon. He has his own "store" on e-Bay, where he sells rare and collectible books.** I'm not an expert in this area, nor is this guide designed to make you one. But it's worth a slight detour to compare Phillip's strategy with the methods employed by a few Amazon sellers. I must advise you, if you decide to pursue this business model, you'll have to buy another book in order to do so.

Phillip makes about $6,000 to $8,000 a month selling books on e-Bay. He says his profit skyrockets during the holidays, since many of the books he sells are either leather-bound, first editions, autographed copies, or volumes that make great gifts. However, one of the biggest distinctions between Phillip's business and those presented in the profiles of Amazon sellers is the time requirement needed to study rare and collectible books before getting started.

Another major difference is the financial investment, since many of the books that Phillip sells for thousands of dollars cost hundreds of dollars to buy. When he's lucky, he finds his books at the same venues frequented by other used booksellers. But he tends to focus more on estate sales and auctions.

Because many rare and/or collectible books predate barcodes and ISBN numbers, a scanner isn't capable of looking them up. So, one of the best options for retrieving information about older books is a Sidekick or Blackberry, since these devices will allow you to look up books by title and/or author. I prefer models that offer a full keyboard, making it easy to type in information without the inconvenience of a numeric structure. But, like many rare and collectible book dealers, Phillip has a good idea of what he's looking for when he goes out book scouting. So he uses a price guide as a research tool, along with a mobile lookup device. But, as I said, this is not my area of expertise. I'm simply an onlooker when it comes to Phillip's habits and practices (although I do ask lots of questions).

Case #4: **Edwin is an ex-librarian who has more than 4,000 books in his inventory**. Because Edwin has so many books in his inventory, he has the luxury of buying books about 3 days a week, for 3-4 hours at a time, while still making a very good profit. Since he's a writer, this is an ideal scenario, giving him time to publish his own work.

While Pat's buying strategy only includes books that have a barcode and can be listed for $17 or more, Edwin has very opportunistic buying habits, resulting in a diverse inventory. Thus, he makes purchases across every genre, buying newer and older books, those that sell quickly with a low profit margin and those that sell slowly with a higher profit margin. But he is an experienced bookseller, who knows how to choose books that will either sell for a small profit before the supply outweighs the demand or sell slowly without becoming outdated on his shelves.

With this buying strategy, Edwin needs a multipurpose "lookup device." So he uses a Sidekick II to retrieve information from **www.bookfinder.com**. Although booksellers who limit their sales to Amazon tend to use Amazon's database to look up information, Edwin sells on multiple sites and Bookfinder.com generates information from many of those sites, so this technique makes sense for his business strategy. He travels a scheduled route between Friends of the Library stores and a Goodwill superstore. He also buys books from online book auctions, which is something I've never done.

Of course, all lines of discussion eventually lead to profit potential. Edwin's profits are about $1,400 a week. Some sellers have a faster turnover than Edwin, but I suspect he could take a few months off from book scouting and continue to be a big earner based on the high-dollar/slow-selling books he has stocked in his inventory.

Don't Tell Anyone, It's a Secret

If you're wondering why I've profiled four men, it's because I meet many more men scouting for books than women. This observation may not reflect what is statistically accurate nationwide. But because this is a nearly perfect option for stay-at-home moms, I'd like to see more women taking advantage of the opportunity. So why aren't more women cashing in? One reason, I suspect, is the way book scouts tend to covet information that might make confidants into competitors.

A case in point happened to me just a few weeks ago when I ran into a female counterpart (a rare event). I was really excited. I had just found a book worth $399 that only cost me $3.99. Naturally, I wanted to share the news with someone who could appreciate it (or so I thought). So I told her about my great find. I wasn't shouting it to the rooftops, as her reaction might have suggested, just speaking at normal volume.

But she immediately went into panic mode at the idea that someone might hear me. Her concern was so over-the-top that you'd think we were talking about the Holy Grail instead of a business opportunity. She frantically scanned the area, looking around as if we were secret agents, while urgently pressing her finger to her lips, advising me to "keep quiet!" This is when I added another word to the name of my guide—secret. Although I understand her concern, in my experience there are enough books to go around.

There Are Enough Books to Go Around

I live in a city that has one of the highest ratios of book buyers per capita in the country; yet, I find that there are still plenty of books to go around. And I'm competing with more aggressive, full-time scouts. So why have I found enough books to go around? First of all, I'm sure that those of you reading this guide are very unlikely to tap into my little corner of the world.

Yes, I have found enough books to support my financial needs. I've done so by traveling a route within a 20-mile radius of my home--the location of which I have no intention of revealing. By the way, when you find your own personal book haven, you too should keep that bit of information to yourself. The simple fact is that no book scout can cover every Goodwill store, thrift store, and other book buying opportunities in every nook and cranny of the world.

Remember the book scout in Goodwill who was so afraid that someone might catch on to "our little secret"? If I didn't mention it before, her parting words were: "Don't tell anyone!" Well, that's the biggest reason there is a shortage of information. Most booksellers want to protect their secrets, believing that your success will interfere with theirs.

Of course there is some truth to this thinking. But other booksellers are less of a threat than one might imagine. Not only is it impossible for any one scout to cover the map of book buying opportunities, no single book scout is ever going to know everything. So, specialize! If you choose a couple of areas to focus on, you will be picking up top-dollar books that don't even hit the radar of other scouts passing them by.

Time to Get Started

So what are the best kept secrets of the book buying business? It's time to find out. Just keep your eye out for the six keys to success, along with the ultimate money-making tool. But first, I want to congratulate you for taking the first step on your journey toward greater freedom. I wish you much success along the way!

Look for These Symbols Along the Way to Discover the Secrets of Success

These symbols were created specifically to set the mood for the journey you're about to take. Scouting for used books is like going on a treasure hunt, especially if you utilize the ultimate money-making tools.

Remember how much fun scavenger hunts were as a kid? Well, think of it as a hunt, and you just happen to have the golden keys.

Or, if you're a gambler, imagine the adrenaline rush you'll get when you find a book costing $2.99 that's worth $399.

It really can be fun; just follow a few simple rules to make the extra cash needed to be a stay-at-home mom.

I PERSPIRATION

First Things First: Getting Started

Signing Up

Signing up to become an Amazon seller is easy. All you have to do is go to www.Amazon.com. At the top of the page you will see the option "Sell Your Stuff." Click on this option. Read through "Top Questions Asked," go to the "Quick Start Guide," sign up for the program and prepare to get started. If you want to become a ProMerchant Seller (which I'll discuss in just a bit), you simply click on "Become a ProMerchant." It's that easy. But not so fast! You will first want to finish reading this guide, build some inventory, and have your packing and shipping supplies ready to go.

Your Business Name

You will also want to put some thought into your online bookseller's name. It is helpful to go to the Amazon website and look up a few books, clicking on the used book option to examine some existing names. Ask yourself questions about whether or not the names you find would influence your buying decision. Do any of the names jump out at you? You might also consider questions such as: what names sound trustworthy or friendly? What characteristics do you want your name to convey? In short, you are establishing an identity for your online bookselling business, so consider it carefully.

A Business Bank Account

You must also decide whether or not you want to open a separate bank account for your funds or if you want to have them deposited directly into an existing account. Certainly, if you want to create a real home business, a separate account is wisest, making it easier to keep track of business expenditures and profits.

Bookkeeping

For major decisions, like whether or not to claim deductions for the business use of your home, you need to consult a higher authority. I simply keep track of my earnings and expenses, record them on an Excel spreadsheet, and transfer the totals to a tax return. You can also visit the IRS website at http://.irs.gov. You will want to familiarize yourself with "Schedule C" guidelines.

How It Works

When an Amazon customer wants a book you have listed, Amazon buys it from you and sells it to the buyer. So Amazon collects the money from the customer. This means that you don't have to worry about doing anything with the customer other than checking your sales each day, emailing the customer to tell them their book has been shipped, and shipping the book promptly.

To find out what books have sold, Amazon notifies you that they have sold the book you listed with them via email. You will also go to your "Seller's Account" and click on "Recent Sales," where you will have the option to click on "Contact Customer," so you can respond to buyers with a confirmation letter (featured in the appendix and detailed later).

Thus, to fill orders you will have to go to your "Seller's Account" on a daily basis. To do so, start on Amazon's homepage, clicking on "Your Account" at the very top of the page. On the next screen, look to the right and you will see "Your Seller's Account." Click on that and it will take you to your account. Once there, look under "Manage Your Orders" and click on "View Your Recent Marketplace Orders." This will access a list of the books sold. You will then click on each order separately, choosing "Print Shipping Label" in order to print the packing slip and label. The packing slip is then cut in two. One section is included in the envelope with the order. The other is a shipping label that you can tape to the envelope. And don't forget to click on "Contact Customer" to tell the buyer their book is being sent.

That's how easy it is! In fact, although this guide has been written to meet the needs of the technologically insecure, more often than not, you can just go to the Amazon website and follow their prompting to get where you want to go.

At the time of this printing, for Amazon's services, a 15% commission is charged on each book sold, along with a variable fee in the amount of $1.35. However, a portion of the fee structure is determined by whether or not you choose the ProMerchant Program. Under the regular program, Amazon also keeps an additional $.99 per book (so you must deduct 15%, $1.35, and $.99 in profit per book). However, the $.99 per book fee is waived if you are on the ProMerchant Program. This program costs $ 39.99 per month, but for most sellers it is well worth the cost.

A big advantage of the ProMerchant Program is that you do not have to re-list books if they don't sell in the first 60 days. As you will discover, some books will be listed on Amazon for longer than 60 days before selling. If you are not a ProMerchant seller, you will need to keep close track of the books you have listed because they will drop off your inventory after 60-days, and re-list them as needed.

The ProMerchant Program is appropriate for anyone selling more than 40 books per month since $.99 x 40 = $39.60. For example, if you list a book for $10, Amazon collects the money from the customer and deducts 15% or $ 1.50 + a $1.35 variable fee. Thus, the net amount you get from Amazon would be $7.15 (+ shipping, which will be covered later).

If you choose not to use the ProMerchant Program, the formula for a $10 book is as follows; Amazon collects $1.50 (15% percent) + $.99 (per book fee) + $1.35 (variable fee), so you get $6.16. Of course, to calculate your net profit you must also deduct the price you paid for the book. Thus, using the ProMerchant Program, a $10 book that cost $2 would be $10 - $2 - $1.50 and -$1.35, which equals a profit of $5.15. You will usually realize an additional profit increase when shipping charges are less than the $3.99 Amazon currently pays you.

In a nutshell, the program with a $.99 per book fee is for casual sellers, and I suspect you plan on selling more than 10 books per week. When you are ready to sign up you will find a complete list of ProMerchant advantages. This will make the first decision simple--the ProMerchant Program is the best option, once you have a couple hundred books in your inventory, and plan on selling more than 40 books per month.

Then, twice a month, Amazon electronically pays you by putting the money you received for all the used books you sold into the bank account that you set up when signing on.

Note: If you need cash before your bimonthly automatic deposit is due, go to Amazon's homepage and click on "Your Account" at the top of the page. Then click on "Your Seller Account," (on the right-hand side of the next screen). Look under "Get Paid," select "View Your Amazon Payments Account & Billing History," click on "View Your Amazon Payments Account Summary," enter your password, and select "Transfer Funds Now." The funds will show up to your account within 5 business days.

> **Stay-at-Home Mom Tip #4:** Choose the ProMerchant option! You don't have time to re-list your books every 60 days, and you're going to sell more than 40 books a month. But wait until you have 2 or 3 hundred before signing on.

Shipping and Handling

As I mentioned, at the present time Amazon pays an additional $3.99 shipping costs for standard media mail (adjustments are made for expedited and international shipping). If you are not familiar with media mail, it is an option available through the United States Postal Service. It is aligned with Amazon's shipping standards, offering inexpensive shipping rates for books, music, and videos. It is recommended that you allow 4-14 days for media mail packages to be delivered. When you list your books you will also have the option of offering expedited or international shipping, in which case shipping credits will be adjusted when appropriate.

As discussed in *How it Works,* using this rate, books weighing under a pound are shipped for $2.31. Books weighing over a pound, but less than 2-lbs., ship for $2.65. If a book weighs 2 to 3 lbs. it costs $ 2.99, leaving you with an extra dollar to cover packing costs. Thus, the lighter the book (like paperbacks) the more money you save on shipping charges, adding a slight boost to profits.

How to Ship Your Books If You're Starting Slow

In the early stages of your online business you can take your packaged orders to the post office, have them weighed and the postage affixed while you wait. This is also your opportunity to get to know the staff at your local post office. This is noteworthy because you will want them to be familiar with you when you are ready to take the next step--printing your postage online.

How to Ship Your Books if You Don't Want to Stand in Line at the Post Office

As you will discover, when your business increases it will become inconvenient for both you and the postal worker to weigh and affix postage while you wait. This is when you will take advantage of the option to buy your postage on the Internet. This allows you to pay for and affix your postage in advance, so you can simply drop your books off at the counter rather than waiting on line. Remember, you know the postal workers, who will be ecstatic because they no longer have to affix so much postage.

Signing Up to Buy Your Postage Online

When you are ready to sign up for this service, go to **www.endicia.com.** Simply follow the instructions to sign up. You will be able to select the level of service that you desire. But it is fine to start with the basic service plan. At this time you will also need to purchase a postal scale to weigh your own packages. In addition to postage, Endicia also charges a monthly fee.

Endicia's current fee structure is outlined below. It's worth every penny.

Billing Period	Monthly	Annual
Windows Standard Plan	Only $9.95/mo	Only $99.95/yr (save $19.45)
Windows Premium Plan	Only $15.95/mo	Only $174.95/yr (save $16.45)
Mac Premium Plan	Only $15.95/mo	Only $174.95/yr (save $16.45)

Once you have signed up for this service a DAZZLE icon will be added to your desktop. This icon will take you to Endicia's postage options. You will be able to buy postage for media mail, first class mail, priority mail, or international shipping. You can even buy insurance to avoid those long post office lines.

When you are ready to print your postage, you will have a delivery confirmation option for 14 cents. Letting customers track their own order, rather than emailing you every few days to inquire about the status, is worth 10 times the cost. Delivery confirmation forms can also be found at the post office, just look for lime green forms or ask where to find them.

Packaging Books

Another cost to be factored in is the price of the envelopes, sealing tape, and any other packing materials. But there is no need to spend a lot of money on shipping supplies. If you are starting out with minimal investment income, you can buy a roll of bubble wrap and wrap each book before putting it in an envelope. Or you can realize further savings by wrapping your books in brown paper, which can be purchased on a roll from any office-supply store.

You can also buy a Costco or Sam's Club box of labels to print return address labels and media mail labels (which I used before I started printing postage online). Just look inside the box for instructions on how to make labels.

As business increases, consider buying padded or bubble-wrapped envelopes, in bulk, to save time. Once you have the luxury of this time-saving bonus, you'll never want to go back!

The packing process is simplified by using the packing list provided by Amazon that can be printed from your "Recent Sales" list. This list includes a shipping tag that can be cut from the top of the packing slip and taped onto the envelope. If you use Endicia, you can print the postage along with the customer's address and your return address all on one sheet that can be taped to the envelope or printed on Avery stickers to save even more time. Instructions are available on the Endicia website.

Then it's off to the United States Post Office!

Building Your Inventory

Of course, none of this can happen without the product--the book. To begin the process of building your inventory, you will need to do a little shopping. First, you will need to learn where to find books. Location ideas can be found under the heading: *Where to Find Books,* while selection techniques and guidelines can be found under: *Selecting Books.* I have also put together lists of books that I have sold from my own inventory, which can be found in the appendix under: *What Books to Buy.* I designed this list to give you a head start. As you'll discover, finding books worth buying requires an eye for value. This ability is developed over time, with practice.

With this in mind, the lists I provided in *What Books to Buy* includes examples designed specifically to reduce the time you will need to spend going through the bookshelves at local stores in order to bring yourself up to speed on book selection. It is basically a study in the *type* of subjects and titles you will be looking for, not a memorization task. Combining specific examples with general guidelines is the best way I know to help you identify those treasures that will keep you going back for more, without taking you out book-hunting myself--which would actually be the ideal method.

Once you know where to look, and have some idea of what types of books you will be looking for, you will also need to know how to determine a book's value and salability, once you have it in hand. Thus, you must learn how to use your mobile lookup device to find the price, availability, and sales rank of a book and know how to put these three pieces of information to practical use. Then you'll be prepared for your first book scouting adventure.

So let's get started learning some of the basic keys to success.

Remember my forewarning about the need to connect all the dots in order to determine a book's *true* value? Well, it's time to get started. You can hit the ground running by learning to implement the first three keys to success: **FIND THE SELLING PRICE OF THE BOOK, FACTOR IN AVAILABILITY,** and **CHECK THE SALES RANK.**

Accessing Pricing Information

Before considering which mobile lookup tool suits your needs, it is important to understand how to use this technology in making informed buying decisions. These are the three pieces of information you will be looking for: price, the number of books available, and the sales rank. The listing price of a book can be found by searching Amazon's database. The method that follows gives you the basics of accessing pricing information from your home computer. Once you understand the method, you should be able to make the slight alterations required when utilizing a mobile lookup tool.

You will begin by going to Amazon.com, clicking on the "Sell Your Stuff" tab located in the top section of the home page. The next screen will say, "Sell your Stuff" and will offer ways to search for a book's listing. Locate the box that says, "enter the ISBN, UPC, or ASIN." Your first choice is to plug the ISBN number into this box. This number can be found on the back of most books or on the inside copyright page.

On rare occasions the ISBN number will yield no results. Or the book may not have an ISBN number. In those cases, go to the box above "Search by ISBN, UPC, or ASIN" and modify your search utilizing the box that says, "Search by Title or Keyword." As the box suggests, you will type in the title or key words, such as the title and the author's name. If that doesn't work, you can search the author's name for all of his or her titles. From here you should be able to make your own way, clicking on the title and then clicking on "new and used copies" to find the used selling price of the book.

Some older books have SSN numbers rather than ISBN numbers. Before searching by title and/or author you can sometimes add a 0 before the SSN number to access information about a book. But be sure to look at the title once you access information by using the SSN, with the leading 0 approach, to be sure you have an exact match. Don't just look at the price and make a quick buying decision (it's easy to make a mistake when you're out in the field rushing to find the best buys).

For tapes and CD's that don't have ISBN numbers, you can use the UPC number to look up information. This number is written along the barcode. Just go to the same box used to look up books by the ISBN number, where it says: "Search by ISBN, UPC, or ASIN," and type in the UPC number. But first pull down the appropriate category in the "product category" box.

Availability

And don't forget availability! Simply take note of the book's availability when looking up the price. This is easy enough to find. Along with the title you will see a number next to the used book price, such as: 61 Used & new from $4.25. This number (61 in the example) is going to help you determine whether the supply will outweigh the demand before you have a chance to sell your copy of any given book. Of course, you will need to know the sales rank in order to make that determination.

Accessing Sales Rank Information
(Go to the Appendix for an In-depth Discussion)

The sales rank is more difficult to find. But taken together the price, sales rank and number of copies available will help you best determine whether or not a book is worth buying. To find the sales rank you will click on the title of a book and scroll down to "Product Details." Once there, you will find a section that looks like this:

Amazon.com Sales Rank: Today: #2,882 in Books

                                                         Yesterday: #3,082 in Books

Sometimes, in order to find the sales rank you must click on the title of the book, then click on "New and Used," where you will find the option "View Product Details." Click on "View Product Details" and scroll down, as detailed above, until you come to the sales rank.

So Now the Buying Process Should be Easy, Right?

Now that you know how to find a book's price, availability, and sales rank, the buying process should be easy, right? The fewer available books the better; the higher the price of the book the better; the lower the sales rank the better. Unfortunately, it's not that simple. The perfect book with a high sales price and a low sales rank is the exception, not the rule. Thus, you will need to delve deeper into the buying process. Probably the most difficult piece of information to factor into buying decisions is the sales rank. So, it's time to review some sales rank basics followed by methods of putting basic information into practice.

The Basics of Sales Rank

Amazon's own perspective on sales ranks can be found in their FAQ section where they close by saying, "I hope you find Amazon.com Sales Ranking *interesting.*" Note their choice of the word interesting rather than informative or useful. In fact, the process of figuring out exactly how Amazon calculates sales ranks is impossible, since the algorithm used is proprietary. However, details that have been extrapolated from research provide enough information to help used booksellers make more discerning buying decisions. Although there is some discrepancy in the research extrapolated by various individuals, it is still of value. But before moving on to some of the ways that sellers might put the information to practical use, here are a few basics.

• When it comes to sales ranks, the lower the better (think of it like your weight). Thus, the lower the sales rank the faster a book is likely to sell.

• Here's how it works. Every book that has ever been sold on Amazon is automatically assigned a sales rank. The number assigned can range anywhere from number one, which represents the latest bestseller, to somewhere in the millions, representing books that have sold at least one copy but are by no means bestsellers. The other possibility is that the book has no sales rank, meaning the book has never sold a copy on Amazon.

• One reason sales ranks should not be taken as absolute determining factors is as follows: a sales rank given to a book that sold thousands of copies when it was a bestseller may be experiencing a residual effect from the initial surge of high sales. This may give a book a lower ranking than it deserves, possibly for many months. Textbooks are especially prone to this problem, so pay careful attention to the special guidelines pertaining to textbooks, offered in the appendix.

• Books that have very high sales ranks are also extremely difficult to use as predictive factors, since one additional sale can improve the ranking significantly, but only temporarily. A good example would be the fact that a book ranked above two million (meaning it has previously only sold one copy) could improve its ranking by 500,000 from just one additional sale. If that one sale was made on or around the day you happen to be looking for its sales rank, it can completely throw off the ranking's predictive nature.

• Therefore, sales ranks are most significant when they remain in the same range for an extended period of time.

• Sales ranks with lower numbers are also more predictive than sales ranks with higher numbers. Since a sales rank in the realm of 1,000 means a book is selling at least ten copies a day, it is unlikely that a few extra sales or the residual effect of past sales will have a dramatic, temporary impact on a ranking.

• Trending projections and historic sales play a key role in determining the rank of titles in the 10,000-100,000 range. If a book is trending upward, a book's sales rank can jump from 800,000 to 100,000 in 24 hours.

Estimations of the Sales Potential of Books Based on Ranking

• A ranking of 10+ means an estimated sale of 100-500 copies each day.

• A ranking of 100+ represents an estimated sale of 10-100 copies a day.

• A ranking of 1,000+ means an estimated sale of 1-100 copies each week.

• A ranking of 10,000+ means an estimated sale of 1-50 copies each week.

• A ranking of 100,000 means estimated lifetime sales exceeding 200 copies.

• A ranking of 1,000,000+ means an estimated lifetime sale total of less than 50 copies.

• A ranking of 2,000,000+ means an estimated lifetime sale of a single copy.

Using This Information to Make Buying Decisions

Now that you've had a briefing on sales rank basics, it's time to put a framework around these indeterminate numbers paired with the subjective process in which they are put to practical use. Not an easy task. But I'll give it a go, beginning with the buying strategies used by a couple of successful booksellers.

Some booksellers use very simple buying techniques. For example, I know a successful online bookseller who only buys books ranked under 500,000, with a minimum listing price of about $24 or so per book. Of course, this is a subjective process. So he makes slight alterations along the way, factoring in availability and condition, while using a scanner to quickly implement his buying strategy. It's fast, it's easy, and he says it works.

Another bookseller is studying for the bar and needs immediate cash to pay his bills. So he limits himself to books ranked under 100,000. Using his strategy, when the profit is only $5 or so the book must be ranked under 10,000. But for books ranked from 10,000 to 100,000, he demands a listing price in the $17-$24 range, and reports that he usually succeeds in selling most of these titles by the end of the month. In the worst case scenario, he would need to go out scouting 5 days a week to find at least 20+ fast-selling books, each time, with a minimum $5 profit to make the $500 a week that he needs to pay his bills (the "+" is to pay for expenses). Of course, this example is for demonstration purposes only and many of the books he finds have a higher profit margin than $5, so he is never required to find 100 + books to meet his quota (thank goodness!). The key to his strategy is fast turnover.

But those who employ a diverse buying strategy can take advantage of the wide variety of books that cross their paths while out book-hunting. For this reason, I will address four distinct ranking schemes, creating a framework in which to address some of the challenges that tend to be inherent to each of these categories.

The 10,000 Top-Selling Books

This is the category associated with high-volume selling of low-profit books. Since a sales rank of 1,000 represents 10-100 copies sold per day, you can expect to sell a book with this sales rank in a day, if not hours. Even at the upper range of 10,000, the estimated sales are 1-50 copies sold per week. With this in mind, although it is theoretically possible to buy a title that's only selling 1 copy a week, in my experience the odds are in your favor.

An advantage of these books is that they tend to be readily accessible, since they are top selling books, boosting the quantities in which they are donated. As mentioned previously, in this fast-selling category I demand a minimum $5 or $6 profit. I am not willing to put my energy into listing, packaging, emailing customers, and shipping a book for any less. I also price these books competitively, so they will sell in less than a week. After all, the main reason for selling low-profit books is the fast turnover.

When selling a high-volume of low-profit books, it's important to remember that you're building your reputation along with your inventory. So don't risk a low rating for a few dollars. My motto is to **under-promise and over-deliver.** Thus, I am conservative when assigning the condition category, and have a full disclosure policy when writing additional comments. I always accept returns, but I more readily give refunds (with no expectation that the book will be returned to me) for these low-dollar books—writing it off as promotion. Remember: when selling online, you're nothing without your reputation.

10,000-100,000 Midrange Sales Rank

As mentioned, some research suggests that a sales rank of 10,000 is representative of weekly sales, on Amazon, ranging anywhere from 1-50 copies, while a ranking of 100,000 represents *total* lifetime sales that *may* be limited to as few as 200 books. Thus, the lower ranking numbers are a safer bet when buying for resale. Also, remember that sales ranks are most predictable, as an indicator of speed of sales, at the lower end of the spectrum.

However, these numbers are not absolutes. So this numeric breakdown is not only based on some available research, it is also rooted in experience and the feedback I have elicited from other sellers. Having said this, many sellers report very good luck selling books ranking up to

100,000, on average, within a few weeks. You will have to experiment with these numbers a bit. But when determining your minimum profit requirement, I would strongly recommend taking into account the extended time period required to sell books in this midrange ranking scheme, compared to the top 10,000 best sellers. Because these books *do* take longer to sell, I personally demand a minimum listing price of about $17-$24 (again, it's a subjective process), allowing some leeway to lower the asking price, if needed, while maintaining a decent profit margin. I also employ the 3x return on your investment rule, as always.

Furthermore, I pay close attention to availability in this category, because of its direct impact on the possibility that you will have to lower your price to the point of diminishing returns before your book has a chance to sell. In contrast to the fast-selling books, which are going to sell in a day or two whether 38 people have them listed or not, I want the availability to be in the lower range for books that may take weeks to sell. At the top of this range, my price and availability criterion becomes more and more stringent, as do my condition standards.

But a good reason for stocking numerous books in this category (assuming the numbers line up) comes from an accountant, turned bookseller, who crunched some numbers based on his own sales. His findings suggest that the $17-$24 price range is the sweet spot in book sales. He believes that two factors come together to create the perfect synergy. First, a listing price that starts at $17 is generally high enough to allow for a few adjustments, in the negative, before a book reaches the point of no returns. And second, a listing price within this range is also within the higher limits of what the average customer is willing to spend. Thus, with any luck, buying books in this category will enable you to send out fewer books, than is required in the low profit scheme, in order to meet your financial goals.

Sales Ranks from 100,000 to a 1,000,000

This may be one of the most difficult buying categories to assess, since some research suggests *lifetime* sales of only 50-200 books. Also, the predictive nature of the sales rank is further decreasing as the ranking number increases. But remember the seller I mentioned, who buys anything ranked below 500,000 if it costs a couple of dollars and has a listing price of about $24 or more. He says this works out great. So I follow his lead when buying in this ranking scheme. However, I use more caution and apply higher standards after the 500,000-600,000 mark. I have seen research (again, it's not definitive, but it's out there) which indicates a sharp increase in the number of days it takes to sell a book when the ranking is above a half million or so. Thus, I often factor in some less objective reasons for buying when the numbers climb over 500,000. For example, in this category I often pass on books that only qualify for an "acceptable" rating. I have found that no matter how many warnings you include in the comment section, the acceptable category is the most likely candidate for complaints (I've actually resorted to describing a book as "NOT A PRETTY COPY!"). Thus, I would recommend that you make condition and availability a high priority in this ranking scheme, since there is a greater element of risk involved.

Sales Ranks Above 1,000,000

A sales rank slightly above a million indicates *total* Amazon sales of about a dozen books. Because you lose so much of the predictive benefits of the sales rank when the number is this high, it's difficult to predetermine how long it will take to sell books in this category. It can take from 6 months to over a year to sell, or it could completely surprise you and sell in a week.

But books ranked in the millions may be one of the best ways to buy low and sell high, since the availability is often low, driving the price up in the first place and making it less likely that the price will be driven down by competitors. It's a simple matter of supply and demand. In this case you only need one interested customer to make a sale. However, it's up to you to determine what kind of return you want on an investment that may take months to deliver. If a book costs a couple of dollars, I don't mind waiting a year to turn it into $40--as I said previously--I think of it like buying stocks.

The key to buying books with high sales ranks is learning to choose books that will not become outdated on your shelves. Guidelines for doing so will be included in the appendix. It is worth the time and effort it will take to go over these tips, since these books will eventually bump up your monthly profits on an ongoing basis.

I've done my best to create a framework around a technique that's rooted in subjectivity and conjecture. But when it comes to sales rank, no matter how strategically you plan sometimes it's not enough. So play around with the numbers a bit and call on your intuitive side.

Here's a Quick Summary of a Diversified Starting Model

• You can keep your sales strong with high-volume selling of books that have sales ranks under 10,000--the lower the number the better. But sales ranks are not absolutes and some research suggests books ranked up to 100,000, on average, sell within a few weeks. The advantage of these books is accessibility and quick turnover.

• While books with a low sales rank and low profit margin are selling, stock your inventory with midrange and high-dollar books.

• If the sales rank is in the midrange, take availability into account. High availability means a faster race to the lowest price, since there are more sellers competing to sell the same book, over a longer period of time. I factor condition more prominently into the midrange category.

• It is less likely that very high-dollar books will have high availability, since lack of supply often drives the price up in the first place. The important factor here is the continued relevance of the subject matter. You don't want these books to become outdated on your shelf. Also, be sure to apply the special guidelines included in the appendix when buying textbooks.

Develop Your Own Model Over Time

You now have some guidelines to consider when developing your own business model. Your model should reflect your family and financial needs. This includes how much money you need to make, how much you can afford to invest, how fast you need to realize a return on your investment, and how much time you are willing to spend buying, selling, packaging and shipping books.

Your model should also take into account your interests and area of specialization, available storage space, and the local availability of used books. Developing your business is an opportunity to celebrate personal and regional strengths and differences. You should also reevaluate on occasion and make appropriate changes as your business evolves over time.

My goal is to work part-time, doing as little work as possible to meet my financial goals. In the graph that follows, you will see a steady rise in profit per book as the high-dollar books in my inventory began to sell on a regular basis. You will also see how I take advantage of the expandability and collapsibility of this business, if you take note of the drop in sales during summer months (other drops reflect personal or family needs).

Stay-at-Home Mom Tip #5:

I have found that 30 or 40 percent of the energy expended yields the first $300 a week in profit. This is the so-called "sweet spot." So if that's all you need to supplement your income, you're in luck. The books needed to make this amount of money seem to jump off the shelves. But based on my experience alone, I've found that the returns, versus effort, go down substantially after reaching that sweet spot.

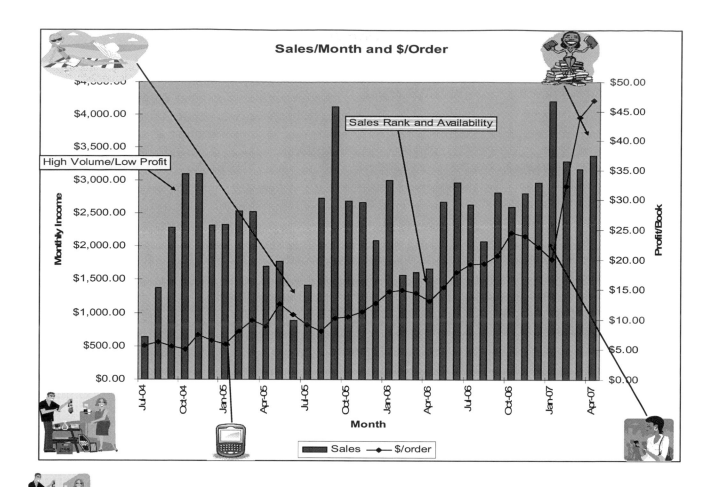

Sales/Month and $/Order

Make a profit ASAP with high-volume sales of quick-selling/low-profit books ($5 in profit per book can still bring in $3,000 in a month).

Set your own hours. Take summers off!

Search the web and factor in sales rank, price, and availability when making buying decisions (I wish I had started this practice before April 05).

Start with the end in sight. I'm building my inventory to eventually make an average of $40 a book and $4,000 a month, working part time.

Work less and make more per hour. I hope this representation helps you plan your own journey to the top of a pyramid of your own design.

Pricing

Although this is an oversimplified explanation of how pricing works, to start you will concentrate on looking for the lowest priced book, in the same condition as the one you are holding when you access pricing information on the Amazon site.

The Fourth Key to Success: List Your Book Competitively

The idea is to be able to **LIST YOUR BOOK AT A COMPETITIVE PRICE--** the fourth key to success. If all else is equal, including the condition of your book and your rating, you want your book to be one of the first books listed in its category, showing up on the screen quickly when a customer does a search. However, don't assume your listing has to be the very first in line. Instead, consider other creative listing methods included in the next section.

Pricing also becomes more complicated when factoring in the following: how many books, of the title you are listing, are already available for sale on Amazon, the sales rank, and the next lowest price. This is significant because you might price your book higher, and sell it after the lowest priced book is sold, if the sales rank is low enough to suggest that the first book listed will sell quickly.

I'll offer an example, not because you can't do the calculations yourself, but because it will give you the opportunity to adjust your thinking to accommodate for the various deductions you will have to consider when making book-buying decisions. It can be easier than you think to end up buying a book that isn't worth your time and effort after Amazon takes its share.

So, here's a quick illustration. If you are holding a "like new" book that cost $2 and the lowest "like new" price listed on Amazon is $20, you can calculate $20 minus 15% (Amazon's commission) = $17-$2 (the price of the book) = $15-$1.35 (variable fee) = $13.65 profit. However, if there is only one "like new" book for $20 and the next "like new" book is $35, you may decide to list your book at $34.99, selling it for a higher profit by waiting until the $20 book is off the table.

Another resource when pricing a book is **www.bookfinder.com.** If I think a used book listed on Amazon has an inflated price, I will compare it with the prices found on www.bookfinder.com before posting my listing (I like to get a great return on my investment, but not by price-gouging). Some book buyers also elect to search bookfinder's database, rather than Amazon's, before buying books. I don't use this method, except in the instance described above, since I have had success using Amazon prices as my main search tool.

Price Wars/Outsmarting Pricing Software

Another pricing challenge is the fact that many booksellers now have software that automatically detects when a competitor undercuts their price. This gives sellers with this software the advantage of a constantly refreshed inventory. So you have to outsmart pricing software to compete.

Some software programs allow sellers to set minimum and maximum prices, while other systems allow for more complex re-pricing configurations. But, in general, I have found it helpful to price my books a few cents higher than the competitor's price, often leaving the software unaware of a new listing.

Another option is to rate a book that you consider in "very good" condition as good and write "good + to very good," in the comment section. This gives you an edge over other books in the "good" category. I believe this is a fair practice (or I wouldn't have included it), because rating a book is a subjective process; thus, I base all my listings on the under-promise/over-deliver motto to keep my customers satisfied. I also like the added bonus of breaking free from the endless cycle of lowering books by a few cents, incrementally, to the point of diminishing returns.

You can also offer free expedited shipping for lightweight or expensive books, if necessary. I say if necessary because this is where a high rating helps. In fact, I recommend maintaining a high rating as the first line of defense. Buyers are certainly willing to pay a bit more to buy a book from someone with a 98% rating versus someone with a 94% customer rating. So if the opposing seller has a discernibly lower rating, the expedited shipping bonus isn't necessary.

Purchasing Software Designed for Amazon Sellers

At some point, your inventory may become so large that the subscription fees associated with third party software may be worthwhile, based on its time saving features. My inventory consists of 1,000-1,200 books at any given time, but I still take a hands-on approach, updating my own inventory on a daily basis and sending out emails one at a time. However, I have looked into third party software, because I'd like to spend more time out book scouting instead of sitting in front of the computer. In truth, as much as I enjoy hunting for books, I dislike going through my inventory every day and emailing customers one at a time.

Third party software systems range in functioning from features designed for the singular purpose of re-pricing books to all encompassing systems that streamline your entire business. On one end of the spectrum are *Re-Pricing Machine* (www.doolicity.com) and *BookRepricer* (www.bookrepricer.com), both offering subscription programs designed to re-price your Amazon listings to the lowest price, so you can be the first in line. At the other end of the spectrum is the *AMan Pro* system, offered by SpaceWare Inc, which has the ability to fine tune re-pricing to your specifications, send out customized emails in bulk, and a host of other functions found at http://www.spaceware.com/resources.htm. Another company offering third party software, along with tutorial training videos, is Seller Engine at www.sellerengine.com.

There is a more extensive list of companies offering pricing and inventory management tools in the index. Just make sure the one you choose only charges a monthly subscription fee. I've heard that some companies also want a percentage of your monthly earnings, if you can believe that.

Listing Your Books

When you are ready to post your books you will simply click on "Sell your Stuff," which is located at the top of Amazon's home page. The next page to appear on your screen will say "sell your stuff," and includes two boxes. The first box is to search for your book by keywords, and the second is to search using the ISBN. Try using the ISBN first, when available.

The ISBN is usually on the back cover or on the inside of the book on the copyright page. If the ISBN isn't available, or fails to yield results, use keywords such as the title of the book. If that also fails, you can combine the title with the author's name, or search the author's name for all titles, clicking on the title in question once you find it.

The next page that will appear on your screen has a pull-down menu where you will select a classification, by using the guidelines provided in the appendix. You will also describe your book, using the same guidelines. The next page that will appear is called "Sell an Item-Enter Price," where you will price your book using information presented earlier.

Note: Because some new sellers are overly anxious for a sale, they may price their listings too low. Thus, I know experienced sellers who prowl Amazon's website looking for resale opportunities. Yes, prowling sounds a bit predatory (especially since I'm guilty of the same), but the sale generated - from one bookseller to another - might help dubious new sellers come to believe in the possibilities. If you are that over-eager new seller, take your time when you are ready to "sell your stuff" so you don't sell yourself short.

Storing Your Books

For the first hundred books, you don't have to be too organized. But once I had over a hundred books in my inventory, I organized them alphabetically, by author. I then separated them into categories similar to those found in a library or bookstore. My categories included: children's books, religion, self-help, psychology, education, parenting, medical, game books, home and garden, text books, fiction, history, foreign language, and miscellaneous.

However, more recently I have chosen to categorize books according to a SKU number. SKU stands for stock keeping unit. Although the listing ID can be used as a SKU, Amazon recommends that you also enter an optional SKU for your records. The SKU is assigned at the bottom of the page, when you price your item for sale, before hitting "continue."

You can assign a SKU to each listing as a unique identifier. A SKU can be up to 40 characters long and can contain both letters and numbers. It will then be included on your packing slip so you can quickly find the item, matching the respective SKU with the item sold. Using this method, books can be organized utilizing the date the book was listed as the first 6 numbers in the SKU. That date can then be followed, numerically, according to the order in which the books were listed on any particular day. You can also follow the number with an alpha-identifier, like B for books or V for VHS tapes, and so on. This way you can stock these items in separate boxes if desired. Here's an example: SKU = 10220601V

10 = month, 22 = day, 06 = year, 01 = 1st book listed on that date, V = VHS

I have found it best to write the first 8 numbers on a Post-it that can be adhered to a storage box. As you begin to sell the books in your inventory, you will be moving books from one box to the next. Thus, the impermanence of numbers being taped to boxes allows you to make appropriate adjustments according to the flow of books. You will simply renumber your boxes as necessary.

Inventory Maintenance
The Fifth Key to Success: Refresh Your Inventory

It's time for the fifth key to success. **REFRESH YOUR INVENTORY ON A DAILY BASIS!** You've already read a few competitive pricing and listing tactics in the section on outsmarting third party software. These techniques allow you to have a certain competitive edge without necessitating that your book be the very first one in line. But you *do* want your listing to be close enough to the top, in its respective condition category, to generate a sale.

Once you ensure that your listing is among the front-runners, you can be creative in the comment section and use your high rating to gain an advantage. However, you must continue to make appropriate adjustments on a daily basis. Failing to refresh your inventory is like throwing money away. Make it a priority! If you have 3rd party software, the re-pricing will be done for you, so you're off the hook.

It also helps to become aware of peak buying times and to be ready for them. For example, because I live on the West Coast, I refresh my inventory first thing, so I don't miss out on those morning sales on the East Coast. There is some research to support early morning on-the-job buying. So, accommodate for time zones and those early morning buyers. While they're sipping a double vanilla latte, they are also browsing the web before they start their day.

Simple Instructions for Refreshing Your Inventory

To refresh your inventory, click on "Your Account" on Amazon's homepage. The next screen has "Seller's Account" in a box on the right hand side of the page. Click on "Seller's Account." You will see "Manage Your Inventory," on the top of the page. Under "Manage Your Inventory," look for "View your Current Inventory for Sale," and click on "Open." You can set your inventory to show a list of your books paired with the lowest priced book in the same condition category. Then go through your inventory, page by page, making appropriate price or comment changes and saving the changes. Or you can purchase software to do this for you automatically if your inventory becomes too large to manage yourself.

Inventory Review

Even if you're a ProMerchant Seller, you need to go over your inventory every once in a while. I do it every six months to a year. The last time I went through my entire inventory, I found that 3% of my books had either fallen off, meaning that they were no longer listed on Amazon, or they appeared to be available, even though I'd sold them. I was especially concerned about those that were actively listed; leaving me open to negative feedback had a customer ordered a book I couldn't supply.

To review your inventory, start with a list of the books you have by going to your account and selecting "Get Listing and Fulfillment Reports." Then select "Generate Reports Now." By clicking on "Open Listings Report," you will be able to generate a report, which will be emailed to you when it is ready. You can then print the report and use it to look through the books in your inventory.

Where to Buy Books

The rule of thumb for buying books--as most guides will tell you--is anywhere you can find them. But start by going to www.booksalefinder.com and click on your state; then refine your search to your area, where you will find sales listed both by date and place. This is an excellent way to find Friends of the Library locations, libraries with ongoing sales, thrift stores, and upcoming special occasion sales in your area. Also go to www.Goodwill.com for names and addresses of stores in your area. And don't forget the yellow pages.

During warmer months, I usually go to a few garage and estate sales in my area. I also like the lack of competition at three of my local Friends of the Library stores, Goodwill store and favorite thrift store, where I buy most of my books. My local library also has a small section containing books for sale (I don't think the volunteer presiding over the fundraising shelves likes me too much, but I haven't given up yet). Special occasion sales also have some great buys. As I mentioned earlier, this experience is just more competitive. These sales draw in many book buyers, often travelling many miles to be first in line, prepared to claim their territory. With this in mind, be sure to arrive early, standing in line for as long as necessary if you want the best values. I know someone who queued up four hours in advance. As much as he complained, he said he would do it again in a heartbeat based on the returns.

And don't underestimate the importance of timing. When looking for good sources to stock your inventory, you can't just drop in once or twice and give up if you don't find a decent buy. I stress timing because your business can truly rise or fall based on your mastery of this one simple concept. And once you have the timing down, don't underestimate the value of discouraging other book scouts from adding your favorite stores to their book-buying route. To do so, you must arrive when the shelves are being freshly stocked and clear them of value. This will help maintain the illusion that "your store" (an expression I use to describe stores I have all to myself) gets dreadful donations. Don't feel too guilty—you're simply sending other book sellers off to find their own nook-and-cranny of the world. However, if the jig is up and another seller is on to your great find, you still have your area of specialization and tenacity to rely on.

A List of Your Suppliers

- Garage & Yard Sales: A spring and summer staple. If you consider the hunter/gatherer paradigm, and think of the male scout as the hunter and yourself as the gatherer, you'll realize why you have the advantage at the yard sale. As a gatherer, you know more about the people around you. So use this information when deciding which sales might be worthwhile. For example, I like to go to garage sales hosted by teachers, therapists, recent college graduates, consultants, engineers, nurses, and those in wealthy neighborhoods. I also look for sales held to raise money for team sports. These sales are held by a diverse group of people joining together to come up with contributions. It seems the bookshelf is often the first place they look.

I read a book on buying and selling books online, by a man who said garage sales are a waste of time. I beg to differ--he doesn't know what he's missing. I've made many thousands of dollars from garage sales alone.

- Estate Sales: These can also be competitive but worth the effort. Don't forget to look for collectibles: leather bound books, first editions, out-of-print children's books and the like. But be careful of musty smelling books. They are unacceptable according to Amazon guidelines. They've been known to taint everything around them.

- Flea Markets: I haven't tried these, but I know some book buyers who have. I think this option is very area dependent. But if you find one, check it out.

- Thrift Shops: It took some time, but I eventually found a thrift store worth dropping in on twice a week—it's one of my favorite stops. Your success here is going to depend on availability. Look in wealthier neighborhoods where you tend to find the best donations. Or drive to college towns in your vicinity.

- Public Libraries: Local library fundraising shelves are often quite lucrative. But I've found that the personnel at some public libraries aren't especially friendly to book resellers. You'll have to make that determination for yourself and then decide whether you want to keep a low profile, or befriend the staff.

- Friends of the Library Sales: Often some of the best buys are found here. At my local Friends of the Library Store, paperbacks are all fifty cents and hardbacks are just a dollar. However, many of these stores are now selling some of their most valuable titles online. This is one reason you will need to develop an eye for books that fly under the radar. It takes some practice, but I've managed to do so and so can you. You'll have a head start by reviewing the section entitled *What Books to Buy* very carefully. Then get into the mindset of a customer and/or a bibliophile and look for subtle signs of value described in the next segment.

- Goodwill: These stores can be pricey, depending on your state. Go to www.Goodwill.org and find locations nearest you.

- Road trips: Some book buyers venture outside metropolitan areas to hit the small-town Goodwill, thrift store, or Friends of the Library store. College towns may be especially lucrative, since the book reading population is hefty.

- Special Occasion/Large Book Sale Events: These are another great way to make money. As I mentioned, the competition is on. So hit the sales floor running. You might want to check in advance to see if scanners are permitted, and be prepared for the competition.

- Any community sale that comes your way—church, school, synagogue.

Selecting Books: The Sixth Key to Success

Now that you know where to find books, you need to know how to select them once you reach your destination. Your ability to find valuable books will be one of the biggest keys to your success. So you will need four sets of instructions to help you get started.

Step One: Book-Shelving Schedules, the Numbers on Coded Price Stickers, Profit Potential, and Learning to Recognize Less Obvious Signs of Value

Knowing when fresh inventory generally hits the sales floors of your favorite book buying haunts is like knowing when the ship is coming in. You can wait at the dock all you like, but if the ship has sailed—well--the ship has sailed. As I've said, TIMING IS EVERYTHING! (Sorry about the shouting, but it's my last opportunity to make this very important point).

Once you have the timing thing down, you can move on to the practice of reading dated or color-coded price stickers for precise shelving information. Why is this so important? This can help you determine how long a book has been available for purchase. I shop at a few stores that have a number of book scouts dropping on a daily basis. So I know that only the most recently shelved books haven't been picked over. Just ask the person shelving the books what method is in use and go straight to the freshest inventory.

Even when you arrive on time and know how to find the most current inventory, a drawback to finding valuable books is the fact that many stores (such as Friends of the Library and Goodwill) are now selling books online, as well as in their stores. Thus, the proprietors and/or those charged with pricing and shelving books try to skim the cream off the top before stocking stores with the residuum. But don't lose hope. If you learn to recognize more subtle signs of value, you will end up walking away with the biggest prize.

So how do you develop a superior eye? Start by putting yourself in the shoes of customers looking for reading material about obscure or hard to find subjects. A standard practice of such customers is to type in key words to see what titles popup. With this in mind, if you develop the habit of looking at books from this angle, you will find titles that those charged with "skimming" often pass over. In my experience, the untrained eye will intuitively look for titles that suggest broad appeal (remember, many of those working in Friends of the Library stores are volunteers, not professional book scouts like yourself). Yet, many of the top-dollar books in my inventory appeal to a very narrow audience. Fortunately, it only takes one buyer looking for a hard to find book on an obscure topic to generate a great sale. So adjust your book buying sixth sense to accommodate that buyer.

Step Two: Specialization, Profit Potential, Continuing Education, Opportunity, and Tenacity

Even if you have the timing thing down and position yourself to get to the freshest inventory before other scouts arrive, there is always an element of luck involved. Regardless of all the good karma you've accrued in your lifetime, for all those good deeds that have gone unnoticed, you won't always be first in line. But that doesn't mean you need to leave empty handed. This is where a specialty helps. If you specialize, you will be privy to gems that fly under the radar, making access to fresh inventory less obligatory (although I'd never underrate its importance). Furthermore, I'm assuming you didn't leave one incredibly boring and tedious job to tackle another. So have some fun! Choose something you love as your specialization and enjoy every minute of time spent looking through the books you love most.

On the other hand, most of us are also in it for the money. Let's be honest. For this reason, I also buy books based on profit potential. For example, I buy older technical books, taking advantage of their ability to bring in top dollar. There's also plenty of money to be made selling used business books, which I'm afraid I've often—unwittingly--left behind for other scouts to find, simply for lack of expertise (one reason there are enough books to go around).

But in my travels, I have found enough business books, with great resale value and very decent sales ranks, to cause me to rethink my failure to bone up on these titles.

This brings up the need to constantly expand your knowledge base. In my case, it was not only business books that I neglected to take advantage of, but history books as well. Then in two hours flat I made enough money to fulfill my weekly profit objectives, simply by going through the bookshelves of a thrift store looking at specialized areas in history. I picked up books like *The Impact of Chinese Secret Societies in Malaya*, and *The French Presence In Cochinchina & Cambodia,* to name a few, and went home happy. By the way, do you recognize the "subtle signs of value" in the nature of these obscure / specialized topic titles?

Opportunity should also factor into your game plan. So, ask yourself what schools or professions thrive in your area. Also keep an eye out for categories of books that seem to be overlook by local book scouts. For example, I have little interest in cooking, yet I buy and sell cookbooks opportunistically, because of a nearby culinary school. I also, haphazardly, discovered obscure sewing titles stashed away in an arts and crafts section of Goodwill. I knew they had been hidden away forever, based on the store's dated price stickers (and this was in a store frequented by every local book scout). So I added this section to my book buying routine.

This is where tenacity comes in. Indeed, I only looked in the arts and crafts section because I was desperate for a good find. Although I lack the adequate aggression required for competition at large book sale events, I do lay claim to tenacity. If I might take this opportunity to boast, I never give up until every possibility has been exhausted. This includes asking myself questions like, "Where is the last place other scouts would ever look?" Or I reassure myself not to give up by insisting that "there is no way, amongst so many books, that there is no money to be made here." I also sit on floors and rummage through bins, finding books in places where other scouts would only pick up infectious disease (I'm shameless that way). But it often pays off with an adrenaline rush when I liberate books worth $100 + that have fallen prey to cobwebs.

And if I go to a store that has been picked clean of every profitable title, including those that usually fly under the radar, I look in another department. CD's are a good place to start (some scouts make an entire business on CD's), or VHS tapes (for all those customers with out of date technology). I also head off to the game department. Since Amazon sells games, so can you. And if you're dubious, check out the game *Cashflow* (created by the author of *Rich Dad Poor Dad)* on the Amazon website. I found it at Goodwill for $5.99 and sold it for close to $200—and that's just one example.

Step Three: Create a "Bestseller List"

A "bestseller list" is valuable for those of you who plan to buy and sell fast-selling titles as a moneymaking guarantee. The idea is to look for books that are on Amazon's bestseller lists (I use the plural because there's one list for the top 100 bestsellers and other lists that are category specific). Naturally, you will be looking for books that have a used listing price high enough to qualify for the fast-selling/low-profit minimum standards set forth earlier or reset to match your own objectives. If the timing is right, and a book has been around long enough for high-volume donations, without losing its profit potential, it's primed for your inventory.

To prepare your list go to Amazon's homepage, find the "shop all departments" logo along the left side of the page, click on "books", located under "shop all departments" and this will take you to the book department. Once you are there, look along the top header where a tab will direct you to "bestsellers," giving you the opportunity to look through the top 100 bestsellers. Along the left hand side of the page you will also have the option to "narrow by category." With this option you can peruse some of the specific categories that are often associated with top-dollar books like: business & investing, industries & professions, consulting (and so on). In each category, write down the titles of books which have profit potential to satisfy your standards, along with the new and used selling price. Commit some of the cover images to memory, if possible.

When you are deciding which books to buy, look at the new selling price and determine what condition and price requirements *you* would demand, if you were the customer, in order to settle for a used copy rather than buying one directly from Amazon. Then calculate Amazon's deductions, along with the price of the book, and apply your minimum return standard (don't forget the 3x on your investment rule).

As you know, if your ultimate goal is to buy low and sell high you must learn to identify books that are not going to become outdated or undesirable while sitting in your inventory waiting to sell. Titles that may increase in value over time are those that remain relevant based on the subject matter. This might include older books on subjects such as architecture, math, physics, law (no, not tax laws of the 1960's), medicine, and engineering. These books are often most desirable if they are written by pioneers in their respective fields, or related to very specific, or obscure subject matter.

Another factor to consider is that these books may be highly desirable or collectible to professionals working in any one of the aforesaid fields. Many of these professionals are now ready to spend hundreds of dollars on a single book written by a major theorist of their particular persuasion, or they may simply want books that dress up expensive bookshelves.

When learning to recognize value in older books consider the following: titles that focus on certain regions of the world; books related to specific historical settings or time frames; or titles that deal with interesting subtopics in some of the major theoretical models of understanding. For example, when applying this guideline to architecture consider the regional and or historical specificity in titles such as *Soviet Architecture, Industrial Architecture of the United States.* In law, an example that encompasses both regional and historical specificity would be *Diefenbaker Legacy: Canadian Politics Law and Society since 1957.* And here's an interesting subtopic combining two major areas of thought in science: *Astronomy-inspired Atomic and Molecular Physics* (Astrophysics and Space Science Library).

When you're ready to list these specialized and/or obscure titles, tailor your listing to the customer who is likely to buy them. Remember this customer may have initiated a search by typing keywords into the computer. But once they've found a listing of interest, they may want to know more than the basic information that's featured on the product detail page. Thus, it's always best to make your listing the most informative and provide an image if possible. Answering lingering questions may very well result in an otherwise missed opportunity for a great sale.

If you've ever passed on a book because you were left scratching your head, unsure if the book was exactly what you were looking for, then you know what I'm talking about. So, put yourself in the customer's shoes both when buying and selling. This is one of the simplest, yet effective pieces of advice I can extend.

And don't neglect to offer international shipping for all those customers living abroad who are willing to pay good money for books written by well-known professors from American universities. I have sold books on physics, written by MIT professors in 1952, to customers living abroad, for hundreds of dollars (to give but one example). My success is probably due to the combined advantage of offering extra details and international shipping. When you are buying a collectible there are three rules of thumb: edition, condition, and scarcity. I'm not an expert in this area, but I can recommend that you try to think like a bibliophile and use your lookup device as backup if you find something intriguing. There are also a few rules for recognizing first editions in the appendix.

Book-Buying Tools
A Must-Have Money-Making Secret

Now it's time to decide how you're going to access the web from remote locations. If you're really strapped for money, you can go out buying books while someone waits by the phone to look up ISBN numbers for you—that's how I started.

But if at all possible, I would recommend an investment worth making—select one of the ultimate money-making tools: the scanner, Sidekick, Blackberry, or phone with Internet access and a subscription lookup tool. Trust me, it will be the best investment you will make, and will probably pay for itself in a week's time, once you are ready to do some serious buying and selling.

LOOKUP TOOL OPTIONS
Scanner and/or Cell Phone Service

For full details on one possibility, visit Scout Pal at www.scoutpal.com and check out their scanner system that adapts to any of the Nextel "java enabled" phones. Scanners are simple and easy to use. You just scan the barcode containing the ISBN or UPC number, and ScoutPal will present concise results, including a summary of market prices and quantities, sales rank, editions and availability, and used/new/collectible details.

If you decide to get the Scout Pal scanner, the price is dependent on whether or not you already have a compatible phone. There is also a subscription fee of $9.95 a month or

$29.85 quarterly (at the time of this publication). You can also sign up for a one-week free trial subscription with no obligation and no credit card needed.

In short, this tool enables you to quickly comb through stacks of books, sorting out the good from the bad. As they say at ScoutPal, "Book scouting with ScoutPal is like hunting with radar." They also have a cell phone "lookup service" if the scanner's not for you. But don't limit yourself to ScoutPal. Many sellers swear by it, since it can fetch information from a few different sources, but it's not the cheapest option.

Another company offering a scanner package is A Seller Tool. You will find full details of their service at www.asellertool.com/phone.html. They too offer both a scanner and a cell phone service with a "lookup tool" feature that allows you to enter the ISBN or UPC into your cell phone for real time pricing, ranking and other detailed information from the Amazon marketplace. This cell phone service works with nearly all cell phones and has a low subscription price of $10 a month (which they claim is the best deal in town). They also throw in a free re-pricing tool with your subscription.

(Another place to look for lookup tools is Book Hero at: www.bookhero.com.)

Sidekick II and the Blackberry

When buying older books, which don't have barcodes, you will need to plug in a book's title and/or the author's name to access information. Remember the scanner doesn't have this capability. Thus, you might consider a Sidekick or Blackberry (there's also a newer model of the Sidekick, if you want the fanciest gadgetry). There's no denying the fact that it's almost impossible to compete with someone using a scanner to work through a pile of books at a highly competitive book sale. But I buy many out-of-print books that predate barcodes and ISBN numbers, which is why I use a Sidekick. I also make my best money this way and have no interest in changing my business model. On the other hand, just because I use a Sidekick doesn't mean a scanner or cell phone service isn't perfect for your model. So don't let my prototype unduly influence you in this regard.

Stay-at-Home Mom Tip #6: If you plan to buy out-of-print children's books, don't buy a scanner. The scanner reads the barcode to access information, but most valuable children's books are older, predating ISBN's and barcodes. If you're considering the collectible market, the same rule applies. However, if your plan is to go through stacks of books, high speed, nothing beats the scanner.

If you are interested in the Sidekick, it is available from T-Mobile. It costs a couple hundred dollars (rebates are often available). It also has a monthly service charge (it costs me about $72 a month), but has the advantage of working as a phone. A number of companies also carry Blackberry style phones, so check with your carrier. If you're tied to a contract with a specific provider, see if you can transfer your contract to one of these devices. Before you make your final decision, consider the advantages of a full keyboard, rather than the inconvenience of using a numeric structure to type in the data needed for information retrieval (it's fine for text messaging, but annoying when out in the field buying books).

Here's a thought for the super-aggressive bookseller. If you're going to use a scanner, why not pair it with an Internet enabled phone, equipped with a lookup service. This way you will be positioned to make the most of the widest variety of book buying opportunities. This includes speed, when needed, and the ability to look up older books (that don't have barcodes), when needed. Now that I think of it, I might try it myself and get back to you with results in my next book. You might also consider looking at the scanners sold on eBay to reduce startup costs. I checked it out today and found some for half the cost of new.

Customer Service

The Seventh Key to Success

Your Rating

The seventh and final key to success, setting you apart from some of your competitors, is **YOUR RATING**. I cannot stress enough the importance of your business reputation. In this business, your reputation is based solely on your rating. Remember, without a good rating you are nothing but a bad risk! With this in mind, there are a few simple steps to obtaining and maintaining a high rating. Describe your book accurately, follow Amazon's packaging guidelines, ship within 2 business days of the order, make contact with the buyer by sending a confirmation letter, and handle refunds and returns promptly.

If you're not familiar with how it works, once a sale is made, your customers have the opportunity to leave feedback about their buying experience. This feedback accumulates over time to determine your rating as an Amazon seller. Every time a customer looks for a used book online they will not only consider the price of the book, they will factor in your rating when determining what book to buy and who to buy it from. If you've haven't noticed, some unfortunate sellers, with low ratings, need to price their books lower than everyone else, hoping that someone might give them a second chance. Personally, as a buyer I wouldn't risk it. In fact, I will never buy a book from someone who doesn't have all points of the 5-star symbol filled to the tip. Although I don't demand 100% satisfaction, which is basically an unrealistic goal, I look for about 97%. Thus, your rating is inevitably one of your biggest selling tools.

Describing Your Book
(Go to the Appendix for Listing Guidelines)

Describing your books in an accurate manner is the first step to buyer satisfaction, which results in positive feedback and high ratings. Remember, the buyer is putting his or her faith in your integrity, and your business will rise or fall based on the reputation you develop by honoring or dishonoring that faith. It is not worth risking your reputation to make a few more dollars by overrating your book. In fact, my rule of thumb is as follows: **under-promise and over-deliver**.

Before listing your books you should carefully review the guidelines listed on Amazon and those included in the appendix for your convenience. Give as much detail about the condition of the book as necessary to ensure that the buyer knows exactly what he or she is getting. Mention any and all flaws, such as inscriptions, margin notes, highlighting, library stamps, and remainder marks. And put the book in the appropriate category based on that description, as dictated by Amazon's guidelines.

As I mentioned previously, another helpful sales hint is to **offer extra details** (beyond those limited to condition) **in the comment section**, especially when selling older out-of-print books. I have also found that simply giving the buyer a bit of extra information is helpful when selling books about obscure subjects, which the buyer may have found by typing in key words about a subject of special interest, rather than a specific and/or familiar title. For example, if a potential buyer is looking for a book about aero-elasticity, and you are selling a book with that title, you can boost your sales potential by offering any information not listed under the book's product details. Try to answer lingering questions to generate a sale. In short, list any details that give your book validity, such as the professor's name and university affiliations. It really helps!

Note: Ending the comment section with "thanks for the purchase" can set the stage for superior customer service. Gratitude sends off its own positive vibe - don't you agree?

Shipping Speed

According to Amazon's guidelines, you must **ship your book within two business** days of purchase. But you might also consider separating yourself from your competitors by shipping within 24 hours of the order's receipt (or 48 hours for Saturday orders). If you decide to go this extra mile, be sure to make note of it when describing your book, and then be certain to follow through on this commitment. I'm sure it makes a difference since many of my positive reviews include remarks about the speed of shipping, ultimately making this one more way to increase your positive ratings.

Confirmation Letters

(Go to the Appendix for a Sample Confirmation Letter)

To send you off on the right foot, an example of a personable confirmation email has been included in the appendix, which you can personalize and use as your own. This initial contact not only keeps the customer informed, it is also an opportunity to **establish a working relationship with the customer**. Thus, it is wise to write a brief letter that not only informs, but also assures the customer that his or her satisfaction is important to you. Be sure the customer also knows that you are eager to work to resolve any issue that causes dissatisfaction.

In my experience, an unhappy customer is more apt to move straight to the review process, leaving a negative comment next to your name, if you have not made this initial contact. And no matter how hard you may try, there will always be unhappy customers, eager to make certain that future customers know the worst about you and your online bookselling business. For this reason, I have come to think of this initial contact as a crucial element in my promotional, advertising efforts, warding off bad feedback in case something goes wrong with the order or its shipment.

Refunds and Returns

(Go to the Appendix for a Sample "Removing Negative Feedback" Request)

In the same vein, I am very liberal with returns and refunds. Again, I will generally ward off a bad review at any price, within reason, even if it means issuing a refund to someone who may not fully deserve one. Also, keep in mind that some customers don't realize that sellers are willing to work with them. In this case, it is worth emailing your customer, who has the option of removing the bad feedback. When you do, make sure they know that you are concerned and sorry to hear that they are dissatisfied. Then offer them the option of a return, a full or partial refund, or whatever is appropriate to the situation. Using this method, I **ask customers to remove negative reviews, making the request personal,** as you will see in the appendix.

To issue a refund, simply go to your seller account and look under "Manage Your Orders," then select "Issue a Refund." You will also need one of the following: the order ID, listing ID, your merchant SKU, or the buyer's email address, in order to complete the transaction. Because it is likely that a customer has contacted you via email, requesting a refund, I usually copy the email address, select buyer email as my option for accessing the account, then paste the email address in the box provided, before clicking on "continue." There is then a pull-down menu, where you select a reason for the refund. You also have an opportunity to send a short email to the buyer, confirming that the money will be issued to their account within 48 hours.

- _Refresh Your Inventory:_ I do this as early in the day as possible. I am on the West Coast and many people do their buying at work, some while drinking their morning coffee, so I refresh my inventory early to accommodate East Coast peak buying hours.

- _Check to See What Books Sold:_ I do this on a daily basis to prepare for shipping within two days. I simply print the packing slip and shipping label, carry it to my inventory (otherwise known as the garage), find sold items, place the packing slip inside book covers, and move on to the packing process.

- _Package Books:_ I package books at night while listening to music or watching TV. My packing process follows an assembly line routine. I pile up the books, take off any stickers, and erase any prices written inside the books. It's not surprising that customers are universally disgruntled if they find $3.99 written on the cover page of a book you are selling for $59.99 (I wouldn't like it. Would you?). Once you make sure there are no signs of your buying price anywhere, take out the Goo Gone and use it to clean up any dust jackets that may need a once-over; cut the shipping labels from the packing slips; and place them inside the cover. I am then ready to wrap the books one at a time. When this is done I put the addresses and stickers on each envelope and secure them properly (this process is simplified with an online postage service!). Once you are secure in the success of your business, treat yourself to bubble wrap envelopes.

- _Weigh Packages and Buy Postage/Then Head to the P.O._ Or, if you don't have an online postage system, take your packages to the P.O., buy postage there, and have it affixed while you wait.

- _Send Out Confirmation Emails:_ Don't forget the role these emails play in high ratings!

- _Check Email and Respond to Customer Questions or Concerns:_ Remedy any problems in the works ASAP (this may include issuing a full or partial refund).

- _Shop For and List New Books:_ Shopping isn't a daily activity. It will be largely determined by how much money you plan to spend and earn—as you know, the two are connected. I usually go out buying 3-4 times a week, for 3-4 hours at a time.

II What Books to Buy

Introduction

When I take people out to teach them the book buying business, it is always surprising to see how difficult it is for a new book scout to recognize value. Invariably, neophytes choose shiny bestsellers of the recent past that have already flooded the market and now have little or no worth. Thus, I began identifying some of the best book finding techniques and strategies I know, in the section of this guide entitled *Finding Books.* But I thought a more radical treatment of the subject would demand a new, more creative approach. So I decided to paint a shaper image of what you will be looking for by pairing those basic guidelines with a list of real titles from my own inventory. This study in subject and title recognition was designed to give you an idea of some of the *types* of books you will be looking for. No need to worry, this is not a memorization task, nor is a pop quiz in the works.

III Guidelines; Including Examples from My Recent Sales

Children's Books

Many of the male book scouts in my area overlook this genre completely. This leaves numerous older and/or collectible children's books lying dormant on the shelves waiting for me to buy them. Thus, I have found tremendous opportunity in this category. Out-of-print titles are often the most valuable. Indeed, it only takes one customer, with a memory of that very special title from childhood, to make a great sale. In fact, it doesn't surprise me that people are willing to spend quite a bit of money in order to read a book from their own childhood to their children. If you keep this image in mind, when perusing the children's section of used bookstores, you will be picking up the most valuable books on the shelves in no time.

Many people also like to collect first edition copies in this genre. Thus, they can be quite profitable, if you can get your hands on them. For example, a first edition copy of the Dr. Suess book *Bartholomew and the Oobleck* is worth about $200 to $300. Other first edition copies of children's books are worth thousands. But don't forget the collectible rule about condition. People want collectible copies to be in very good condition, with no inscriptions or other markings, and they should include the dust jacket when applicable.

Children's Books I Have Sold Recently

- *Big Alfie Out of Doors Storybook*, used price: $23.99
- *The Rainbow Goblins, used price: $48*
- *When I Was Young in the Mountains* (Fairytale Foil Books), used price: $94.45

Professional and Technical Books

For the sake of discussion, books that have been published for professionals might be divided into two categories. The first category would include newer professional/technical books, which can be difficult to come across since they are likely to be of continued use to the original owner. But the second category, which would include *older* professional/technical books, is where I put substantial effort, since these books *do* become available. Furthermore, they often fly under the radar. So these books are one of the best ways I have found to buy low and sell high. If you can't find a buyer for these books in the US, you can frequently find one by offering international shipping.

Professional books differ from textbooks. However, in this particular context there is a slight exception from the rule since many valuable technical books, which I sell, were once college textbooks. But, the books I'm talking about are not 2004 edition textbooks that have been outdated by the 2007 edition. Instead, they are books written decades ago that remain relevant and desirable based on a few factors that will act as your rule of thumb.

These factors are as follows:

- *continued relevance of the information (like math and physics)*
- *credentials of the author*
- *university affiliations*

- *limited availability of specialized subject matter (like Gem Elixirs and Vibrational Healing)*
- *associations with a pioneer in a field*

It also helps to recognize some of the publishers who are strongly associated with technical books. So start keeping a list of technical books, you find, which tend to be worth money. But first a cautionary note. While some titles in a particular series may be highly desirable, others, in the same series, may be of no worth. So don't make assumptions based on publishers alone (you have a lookup device for backup). For example, *Nuclear Chemical Engineering*, in the McGraw-Hill Engineering Series in Nuclear Engineering, published in 1981, is worth about $1,000. But *Nuclear Power*, in the same series, is only worth about $12. Some examples of highly regarded publishers are as follows:

- *McGraw-Hill Engineering Series*
- *CRC Press Series*
- *Wiley Series in Systems Engineering and Computer Science*
- *Springer Series in Systems Engineering and Management Design*

Also, look for titles that suggest specialization like those that follow:

- *Granulation Technology for Bioproducts (CRC Press Series: published in 1991, but worth ~$95)*
- *Nuclear Chemical Engineering (McGraw-Hill Engineering Series in Nuclear Engineering: published in 1981, but worth ~ $1,000.)*
- *Food Engineering Series: Handbook of Food Processing Equipment (~$140)*

Books that are designed for professionals seeking certificates in their field are often worth a good deal of money, as well. But these must be current, so they may be difficult to find. However, I wouldn't bother mentioning them if I hadn't made good money on them in the past. Your "bestseller list" might help you in this area.

Remember: If you are a ProMerchant you can create new product pages. This is very useful when selling older technical books that may not have an existing listing. The opposite problem may also arise and you may find multiple listings of the same book. In this instance, I try to find the listing with the lowest sales rank and list my copy under that listing. Or I create a listing with an image of the book, if one doesn't already exist (these images do help to generate sales).

Newer Professional and Technical Books I Have Sold Recently

- *The 5 Minute Veterinary Consult: Canine and Feline*, used price: $69.73
- *The Bartender's Book: A History of Sundry Alcoholic Potations, Libations, and Mixtures*, used price: $84.01
- *Oral Radiology: Principles and Interpretation*, used price: $50.99
- *Optics for Clinicians*, used price: $39.99
- *Pain Clinical Manual*, used price: $32.99

Older Professional and Technical Books I Have Sold Recently

- *History of Medicine, 1947*, used price: $50
- *Aircraft Structures, 1950's*, written by Penn State Dept. Head of Aeronautical Engineering, used price: $40
- *Granulation Technology of Bioproducts, 1995*, used price: $95

VHS Tapes

I paid as little as 25 cents for most of my VHS tapes. These are turning out to be a good investment, as more and more video stores fail to stock them. I'm just beginning to appreciate the profit potential of these tapes so you'll have to do some of your own field work to expand your knowledge base when it comes to VHS tapes. But I've already discovered that PBS tapes tend to be of value.

The same is true of educational videos with titles like: Hiking the Grand Canyon, Exploring the Outback, Teenage Pregnancy, Teenage Drug Use, Teenage Driving Safety, and Care of Diabetes. It seems that many educational facilities still have VHS players. And they are often willing to pay a very decent price to present educational subjects in a classroom setting. Here's an assignment for you. Go to Amazon.com and look up the VHS tape Really Rosie. Then decide if you want to add VHS tapes to your inventory. I've sold at least three of these videos.

VHS Tapes I Have Sold Recently

- *Roots (6pc), VHS, used price: $29.99*
- *American Experience: Daughter From Danang, VHS, used price: $19.99*
- *PBS Born to Trouble: Adventures of Huckleberry Finn, used price: $42.50*

Collectibles and Out-of-Print Books

When you are buying a collectible there are three rules of thumb to keep in mind: edition, condition, and scarcity. Because a collectible is often a first edition or out-of-print copy, it makes the rules regarding scarcity and edition a given. But you must also consider what you would be looking for if you were buying a collectible book—which would probably include a greater degree of quality than generally expected when buying a used reading copy on a subject of interest.

In fact, I can assure you that people who are looking for collectibles often don't want an inscription from someone else on the cover page. Nor do they want library stickers or markings of any kind in the text. What they do want is a dust jacket and a book that is in "very good" or "mint" condition (or at a minimum a good, solid, clean copy).

I admit, I don't venture into the rare book category much, since I'd be competing with too many old-timers who know more about these books than I do. Indeed, dealers who put a lot of time and effort into learning about these books know all about the little differences or *points* that make one copy more valuable than the next. They study price guides, and choose areas of specialization. And whether they specialize in biographies, science fiction, modern lit, or something else altogether, they learn everything they can about their niche.

Furthermore, buying rare books or collectibles is not as easy as plugging an ISBN number into your search engine. This area of book buying has a much steeper learning curve. In fact, being a rare book dealer, in the truest sense, is much like belonging to a secret society, exclusive club, or subculture. It's a whole different world!

But buyers who specialize in this area have a lot to rave about. I read that a lot of the money to be made in reselling books comes from collectibles, and that 99% of the money in collectibles comes from first editions. Not much of a surprise, is it? Can you imagine finding a signed first edition copy of Beatrix Potter's *The Tale of Peter Rabbit*? If you find this tantalizing, don't let my lack of expertise in this area stop you from pursuing a specialization in collectibles. Buy a book on the subject and start reading!

Some collectors not only buy out-of-print titles and first edition copies, they also look for the following types of books: leather bound titles, autographed copies, limited editions, and editions that are simply known as the nicest version of a particular book ever printed.

And don't forget Amazon's guidelines, which call for a book to have a dust jacket if it is rated "very good." It astonishes me when I see books listed in "very good condition," followed by a note in the comment section saying "no dust jacket/ minimal highlighting/ and/or underlining." This practice will never fly with collectors. Many collectors are very fussy buyers by nature. Thus, they will not allow for such indiscretions. So take the under-promise, over-deliver motto quite seriously when selling in this category.

Although I'm not an expert in determining the desirability of a certain edition in a certain condition, I do buy many books that garner collectible *like* prices because they are out-of-print (no not 7 & 8 figure prices, but 5 & 6 for sure). As I've said over and over again, I find many of these older books readily accessible and best for buying low and selling high.

Out-of-print and Limited Edition Books I Have Sold Recently

- *Dune Messiah, first edition, $56.90*
- *Remembrance of Things Past, Volume 1-3 Box Set, out-of-print, used price: $49.99*
- *The Complete Far Side 1980-1994 (2 vol. set), used price: $79.99*
- *Cars of the Fabulous '50s, the Sizzling '60s, the Sensational '70s (3-Volume Boxed Set), limited edition, used price: $89.99*
- *Onefivefour, out-of-print and rare, used price: $159.99*

Textbooks

Valuable textbooks are hard to find. On the other hand, if they're current editions they, can be worth a lot of money, so you should know how to determine their worth. In the case of textbooks, plugging an ISBN number into your Sidekick and checking the sales rank isn't a definitive indicator of salability, since the number may be inflated by high previous sales.

So the procedure to follow begins with looking at the copyright number to see how often the book is updated. For example, when you see copyright 1999, 2002, and 2005, you know a new edition comes out every 3 years (unless something dramatic has occurred relevant to the subject matter). Thus, it's reasonable to assume that the fourth edition will be printed in 2008. With this example in mind, if it is late in 2007, it is possible that the textbook has a fairly good sales rank because of sales that occurred over the previous 3 years. However, the book may be on the brink of being outdated and replaced with a newer edition. Thus, if it's a close call, search to see if the 2008 edition has been released. If not, you need to consider how likely it is that the next edition will come out before the next school semester.

Textbooks I Have Sold Recently

- *Patent Law and Policy: Cases and Materials, used price: $59.90*
- *Print Reading for Construction: Residential and Commercial, used price: $41.99*
- *The Professional Chef's Techniques of Healthy Cooking, 2nd Ed., used price: $26.99*

Art and Architecture

Art books are some of the most enjoyable books to buy. But in this category you can't judge a book by its cover, or its contents. Beautiful art that has been set before you on the printed page doesn't always translate into dollar signs.

In fact, books displaying the artwork of some of the most well known artists of all time are often the least valuable books, including those featuring paintings by Rembrandt, Picasso or Norman Rockwell. For example, Abram Art Books are usually quite beautiful and look like they're worth a day's wages; yet, they are usually not worth the price of postage. Thus, high-quality illustrations aren't enough. What sells in this category is often an unusual title; dense text to go with the illustrations; ethnic art; or specialized areas in art. For example, Mark

Ryden, whom I had never heard of, has a couple of books to his credit worth a decent sum. I found one of his books, entitled *Bunnies and Bees,* for $1.99 at a Friend's of the Library bookstore, which is worth about $100. Another of his books, *Wondertoonel,* is also worth more than $100, even though it is a thin paperback.

It's a bit more difficult to pin down high-dollar architectural books, but start by looking for architectural books that focus on certain regions of the world, like *Australian Architectural Form, Exploring China's Architectural Past, Pioneers of Soviet Architecture,* or *Industrial Architecture of US* (1998), these sell for $150 to $500+.

Art and Architecture Books I Have Sold Recently

- *Yunnan School: A Renaissance in Chinese Painting (Hardcover), used price: $399*
- *Weaving China's Past, Amy Clague Collection of Chinese Textiles, used price: $37.50*
- *Sun, Wind, and Light: Architectural Design Strategies, used price: $30*

Game Books and Strategy Guides

I have found that these books sometimes become valuable when they're out-of-print—it's as simple as that.

Game Books and Strategy Guides I Have Sold Recently

- *Official Nintendo Pokémon FireRed Version & Pokémon LeafGreen Version Player's Guide, used price: $42.99*
- *Brady Books Chrono Cross; Official Strategy Guide (Playstation), used price: $85*
- *Universe X, Vol. 2 (Earth X 3), used price: $34.99*
- *Zelda: The Twilight Princess, by Nintendo, used price: $35*
- *Kingdom Hearts 2 Official Strategy Guide Playstation 2, used price: $129*
- *Dungeons & Dragons Core Rulebook Gift Set (Hardcover) used price: $45*

Don't Forget: You're Not Limited to Books
CD'S, Audio Books, and CD Roms I Have Sold Recently

- *Kashtin CD, used price: $84.97*

- *Sid Meier's Alpha Centauri Planetary Pack, CD-Rom, used price: $115.25*

- *Jesus Christ Superstar CD, used price: $22.99*

- *Thai [Audiobook] [Unabridged], used price: $69.92*

- *Fruit of the Spirit, by Joyce Meyer on 10 Audiocassettes, used price: $23.39*

Random Categories

- *Before the Animation Begins: The Art and Lives of Disney's Inspirational Sketch Artists, used price: $54.99*

- *Livestock Judging, Selection & Evaluation, used price: $24.99 (specialized subject matter)*

- *The Student's Pilot's Flight Manual: From First Flight to Private Certificate, used price: $44.99 (certificate program)*

- *Volkswagen: A Week at the Factory: sold for $64.32 (coffee table book)*

- *Conversaciones Con Dios: sold for $100 (foreign language set)*

- *Hindeloopen, A Traditional Dutch Folk Painting Form: sold for $99--(sewing section)*

- *One Circle: How to Grow a Complete Diet in less than 1,000 sq. feet: sold for $65 (unusual subject matter)*

IV What Books Not to Buy

- *Mass market editions, especially popular in the romance section: usually small paperbacks*
- *Advance reading copies: these are ineligible for sale on Amazon.*
- *Books with broken spines, missing pages, or a musty smell: also ineligible for sale on Amazon*
- *Books too heavy to ship,: for example, those beautiful coffee table books which I have had very little success selling in the past.*
- *Outdated editions: such as outdated textbooks*
- *Computer Books: look them up because they are quickly outdated*
- *Encyclopedias*
- *Reader's Digest and Book Club editions*
- *Books which have saturated the market*
- *Textbooks: consider when the next edition is due, not just sales rank*

New: A brand-new, unread copy.

Like New: A book that looks unread, in perfect condition, including a dust jacket. I always ask myself this question: would I be comfortable presenting it as a gift?

Very Good: A copy that has been read, but remains in excellent condition, with a dust jacket (DJ). I usually describe a "very good" book as a clean, sturdy copy. The spine must be in excellent condition and there cannot be notes or highlighting in the book (this includes inscriptions). I tend to keep some bookplates on hand, especially for more expensive books, so I can cover inscriptions, giving the customer an added touch of service. But they still must be listed as having an inscription.

Good: A copy that has been read but remains in clean condition. The pages and the cover must be intact. If the DJ is missing, but there is a pictorial cover, which replicates the preexisting DJ, I make note of this (especially if you don't know if the book was issued with a DJ). Although the spine must be intact, it can show signs of wear, in which case I might describe the book as having edge wear. The book may also include limited or minimal notes and highlighting. Inscriptions also degrade an otherwise "very good" copy to "good." Ex-library books also fall into this category, in which case I make note of library stamps and pockets to insure the customer knows what they are getting.

Acceptable: A readable copy. All pages including the cover must be intact (the dust cover may be missing). An acceptable copy may include considerable notes. I make note of whether the markings are in pen or highlighter, but the notes cannot obscure the text.

Unacceptable: Moldy, badly stained, or unclean copies are not acceptable for sale. Books with missing pages or obscured text are obviously also unacceptable. Also, look out for books that are distributed for promotional use, including advance reader's copies or uncorrected proofs; these too are prohibited for sale.

Listing Books Appropriately: Along with the guidelines outlined above you must also be certain that you are listing your books exactly as they appear in Amazon's database. To do so, you must match your book with an ISBN number, or utilize the title, author, and publication information (including the correct date of publication), if the ISBN number is not available.

If you are a ProMerchant seller and cannot find an exact match, you have the option of creating a product detail page. Just go to your seller account and click on this option. This is a means of listing a product in the Amazon.com stores that is not currently available. When listing a book it helps to include an image.

It is also advisable to detail other helpful information in the comment section. This option can be very useful when listing some of the older technical books that I sell extensively. A key to success is to look at the words contained in the title, and consider the likelihood of key words being utilized as search criteria. I have done very well in this area when I find very specialized books on subjects that are not covered extensively. Give it a try—it might surprise you!

Listing Terminology

After rating books, you will have the opportunity to add further comments about their condition. Booksellers use slightly different terms to describe books, but the definitions below include some general guidelines that will come in handy. If the descriptive word seems too obscure or unfamiliar, combine or substitute it with the definition itself. Whatever you do, don't leave the buyer unaware!

Average Wear - I use this term to describe a neutral book that is in good condition with no defining flaws, inscriptions, or markings of any kind, yet it is lacking in those crisp pages associated with books that are in very good or like new condition. It might also have a limp quality, often associated with books that have been read numerous times throughout the years.

Bowed - When the covers or boards of a hardcover book turn inward toward the leaves or outward away from the leaves it is bowed.

Bookplate - A pasted-in sign of ownership is called a bookplate.

Bumped - When the corners of a book's cover are pressed inward they give the appearance of being bumped.

Chipped - When small pieces are missing or frayed, either on a dust jacket or paperback, the term chipped is applied.

Cocked - When the front and back covers are not aligned--most visible when the book is laid flat--the book is cocked.

Cracked - When you open a book and see that the front or back hinge is breaking loose from the binding it can be described as cracked. You will often notice what looks like netting where the binding is exposed.

Darkening- - When book covers are exposed to light and the color darkens or becomes more intense, rather than fading, the obvious descriptive term is "darkening."

Dampstained - When moisture causes a light stain on the cover or pages of a book it is sometimes called dampstained. *(I suggest using the more familiar term "water stained")*

Dog-eared - When book pages have been folded over at the corners they are dog-eared. If only the creases remain you might describe these as "the history of dog-eared pages."

Edgeworn or ***Edge-wear*** - When there is wear along the edges of hardback book covers or dust jackets they are edgeworn, or have edge-wear.

Elephant Folio - A book that's about 23 inches tall is called an elephant folio.

Endemic Soiling - A term sometimes used to describe soiling that is common or natural to books with use over time is endemic soiling.

Fading - This is the obvious descriptive word used to indicate that the color of a book cover has faded or become less intense due to light exposure.

Foxed or ***Foxing*** - The brown spots, specks or splotches of discoloration on a book's pages, which are commonly brown or yellowish in color, are collectively called foxing (often caused by a chemical reaction in older books).

Gentle Readings (or the signs thereof) - I use this term almost synonymously with "average use." However, one defining feature I look for when deciding which term best suits the visible clues provided is the presence of indentations or imprints left by the turning of pages, or the small fingerprints of a child, who hold the pages too tightly or too long (*an image I embrace*).

Gilded Edges - This term applies to the edges of a book's pages when they have been trimmed smooth and gilt or gold has been applied either in leaf or powder.

Inscribed - When a book is signed either with an inscription to a specific person or with a brief notation along with his signature, it is inscribed.

Limp - An adjective describing a flexible binding in suede or imitation leather is limp.

Loose - When a book is new, the binding is tight, so the book does not remain open to any given page. With use the book's binding becomes "loose," so when you lay it flat it will remain open to any page in the book.

Marbled - This describes paper decorated with an imitation marble pattern.

Moisture Damage - A common term for a variety of signs that a book has been exposed to moisture, denoting more widespread damage than a water stain or dampstained, such as rippling of the pages.

Not A Pretty Copy! - This is not a technical term (but you knew that!). However, it is sometimes what's needed for full disclosure. You might consider using this stern warning if you have a heavily marred book, full of highlighting, margin notes, doodling, and random splashes of coffee, as long as it has no missing pages or obscured text, and lots of important information inside. There are students out there (for example) who are forced to buy books they don't want to read anyway for the going rate of $100, who will gladly deal with all the book's imperfections if you make them an offer they can't refuse.

Price Clipped - When the price has been clipped from the corner of the dust jacket it must be noted as price clipped.

Remainder Marks - When the publisher marks the bottom edges of books sold as remainders with a stamp or black marker, or speckles the bottom with spray paint it is called a remainder mark.

Rubbing - This term is often used to describe a book's cover when the luster of its glossy surface is uneven, causing a slightly smeared appearance (the book looks otherwise new).

Shaken (not stirred) - When a book's pages are beginning to come loose from the binding it's called shaken, but it's probably best to describe the condition in detail, rather than using this unfamiliar adjective.

Slipcase - This is a cardboard case called a slipcase; it is made of cloth or leather. It holds books within it, exposing only the spine.

Smudging - This is another term used to describe a glossy cover that has areas of diminished luster as if rubbed with varying intensity in a circular motion, or smudged.

Soiling - This term refers to stains that are more than slight or endemic. If at all possible identify the source of the same (i.e. coffee). *(If stains are extremely unpleasant--i.e. blood--I would suggest not listing the book at all. In general, I don't mind the other "S" words, like smudged, or sunned, even shaken, but I try to avoid soiled books unless it is most benign.)*

Spine - This is the word used most appropriately to describe the book's backbone—its spine.

Sunned - When a book is faded from exposure to light it is sunned.

Tooling - This is the decoration of a binding. Tooling suggests a degree of added craftsmanship.

Uncut - The term used to describe pages of a completed book that have not been shaved down to a uniform surface is uncut, giving a slightly serrated appearance *(which can actually be quite lovely)*

Water Stain - When a book cover or a page or two are stained from water or other liquids, in a way that can be pinpointed to a general location, it is a water stain. *(I suggest using either water or moisture damage as a description to denote widespread damage resulting in rippled, wavy and/or limp pages)*

VI Confirmation Letter

Hi Jordan:

Just a quick note to let you know I received your order from Amazon Marketplace. Thanks so much for your purchase! I have just packaged your book and will take it to the United States Post Office first thing Tuesday morning *(add the date),* for shipment via USPS Standard Media Mail, shipping from Portland, Oregon. (*Add your delivery confirmation number if you have one.)*

Please allow 4-14 days for arrival. Although unusual, on occasion it can take up to 21-30 days for delivery, especially if you are outside the continental U.S. or have an APO address.

I want you to be happy with your buying experience. So if you have any problems, questions, or concerns, please do not hesitate to email me at...Please include your name and order number in your correspondence.

If you are happy upon receiving your order and have some time to leave positive feedback, it would be greatly appreciated.

I hope you enjoy your book!

My Best Regards

VII Removing Negative Feedback

Dear Mallory,

I am so sorry that you weren't satisfied with your purchase. I value my customers and would like to work with you to resolve this matter to our mutual satisfaction.

Fortunately, the feedback system is designed to promote communication between the buyer and the seller, with hopes that problems might be resolved without need of further intervention. This includes the opportunity for me to issue a full or partial refund. *(Other options include offering the customer another copy of the book, or whatever compromise you're willing to extend in order to keep your rating high).*

Once I have demonstrated my commitment to your satisfaction, you have the opportunity to remove the negative feedback. I know that you have been inconvenienced enough, but it would certainly mean a lot to me if you would consider this option *(remember to make your request personal).*

Again, I apologize for *(whatever it was that went wrong)*, and I want to thank you for giving me this chance to rectify the situation.

My Best Regards,

Instructions for Removing Negative Feedback

If you've left negative feedback on a Merchant seller and have resolved the problem with the seller and would like to remove the feedback, you can do this through "Your Account."

1. Go to http://www.amazon.com/your-account.

2. Find the pull-down menu next to "View by Order." Select "Orders placed in the past 6 months," and hit the "go" button.

3. After you sign in, you'll find a listing of your recent orders. Select the relevant order and click the "View order" button.

4. You will find a feedback section 2/3rds of the way down the page. To remove negative feedback, click on the "Remove" link in the feedback section of the order summary.

5. You may only remove feedback if it has been 60 days or less since the feedback was left.

Thanks Again!

VIII General Guidelines for Identifying a First Edition

Identifying first edition books can be difficult, since publishers identify their books in numerous ways. If this is an area of special interest, you will need to do further research. Consider buying the guide by Bill McBride, which was recommended earlier. But I've included a few general principles to get you started.

A stated first edition is the easiest to recognize because it is written on the copyright page. For example, it will say "First Edition," "First Printing," "First Published," or "First Impression." Another means of identification is when the date on the title page is the same as the date on the copyright.

The number line is one of the most common in use. But not all publishers use the same system, so it is not an absolute. Generally speaking, if the number 1 is present in the line, the book is a first edition, first printing.
For the second printing the 1 is removed. Thus, the number 2 will become the lowest number present.   It might look like this 2 3 4 5 6 7 8 9.

Sometimes a number line is accompanied by a date line. For example: 7 6 5 4 3 70 71 72 73 74 indicates a third printing, published in 1970.

IX Pricing and Inventory Management Tools

- *http://www.spaceware.com/resources for AMan Pro*

This is an all-encompassing program to streamline your business.

- *www.doolicity.com for Re-Price Machine*

This system is geared toward re-pricing books in your inventory so you're first in line.

- *www.booksku.com*

They offer a multitasking software program for Amazon sellers.

- *www.fillz.com*

An online inventory management and fulfillment system for Amazon sellers

- *www.pragersoftware.com*

They have several different options for inventory management and re-pricing.

- *www.sellerengine.com*

They have software for Amazon sellers and tutorial videos for easy learning.

- *www.bookrepricer.com*

An automatic re-pricing tool for Amazon sellers

- *www.sellermagic.com*

Another third party software system designed for Amazon sellers

X Important Online Sites

- *Sign up to become an Amazon Marketplace seller at www.amazon.com*

- *For information on scanner systems or phone service with Internet access, go to ScoutPal at www.scoutpal.com*

- *Another popular Scanner and Internet phone service provider is A Seller Tool at www.asellertool.com/phone.html*

- *Also be sure to comparison shop for the right "lookup tool" at www.bookhero.com*

- *Buy postage online at www.endicia.com*

- *Find the price of books being sold on sites other than Amazon at www.bookfinder.com*

- *Another resource for finding pricing information is Fetch Book at www.fetchbook.info*

- *Find nearby Goodwill locations at www.goodwill.org*

- *Comparison shop for bulk office supplies at www.froogle.com*

- *Find out where to buy used books at www.booksalefinder.com*

Notes